Pre-publication REVIEWS, COMMENTARIES, EVALUATIONS . . .

"**B**ertolino and Schultheis pack a treasure trove of solution-oriented exercises into this exciting, change-promoting book. Clinicians who strive to be effective and efficient will find a lifetime of clinical wisdom at their fingertips. Supervisors and educators can use this book to boost the helping IQ of supervisees and students significantly. The authors have organized the book into sections that contain exercises intended to help clients, family members, *and* therapists get clear on the type of change they desire, alter how they view the problem, modify the doing of the problem, change the context of the problem, and sustain change once it has been achieved. The crystal ball and time machine exercises designed for adolescents are wonderful. Psychiatrists, psychologists, social workers, counselors, nurse clinicians, and other mental health professionals can use the exercises in virtually any type of setting with individuals, groups, and/or families. This book is like a set of power tools that get the job done better and faster. At the same time, they enhance the clinician's enthusiasm, creativity, and ability to collaborate with clients."

Jay Memmott, PhD
Department Chair and Director, MSW Program,
Washburn University, Topeka, Kansas

"**B**ertolino and Schultheis have done a wonderful job of integrating a wide variety of resource- and competency-based ideas and techniques into dozens of clear and practical, easy-to-use exercises that will be valuable keys for moving from problems to solutions. If you want to know how to do what successful solution-oriented therapists and clients actually do, this is the book for you."

Michael F. Hoyt, PhD
Author, *Some Stories Are Better Than Others,*
Brief Therapy and Managed Care, and *Interviews with Brief Therapy Experts;*
Editor, *The Handbook of Constructive Therapies* and *The First Session in Brief Therapy*

"**T**here are times when I hear the words 'notebook' and 'exercise' in relation to the therapeutic process and I cringe. This is because I am worried that I am going to have to deal with a technique-driven and predictable group of exercises that are more likely to detract from the therapeutic process than help. When I read *The Therapist's Notebook for Families* by Bertolino and Schultheis, I realized that I need to change my assumptions related to these words, and think more out of the box.

Both beginning and advanced therapists will find this creative group of exercises extremely helpful in their work. In my view, the strength of the exercises lies in their strong theoretical and empirical grounding in the collaborative and competency-based approaches to change. They are not merely 'neat activities' that Bertolino and Schultheis thought up one sunny day. Rather, each exercise has a clear strategy based upon what works in helping families and adolescents change. This workbook is so much more than an assortment of therapeutic tools. It provides both the therapist and the client with a means to define change, generate solutions, establish alliances, explore alternatives, think in different ways, try new activities, change meaning, augment change, and many more valuable therapeutic effects.

In reviewing the book, I was reminded of the many different ways one can think about problems and their solutions, and how, at times, parents, adolescents, and families are stuck simply because they are unable to see their way beyond their problems. In this work, Bertolino and Schultheis are very effective in providing many different strategies to help parents, adolescents, and their therapists to open up the space needed to define the change they want, to view the problem in a different light, to engage in change-oriented activities, and to generate momentum in the direction of change. I highly recommend this work for all change-focused clinicians."

Adrian J. Blow, PhD
Assistant Professor, Department of Counseling and Family Therapy,
Saint Louis University, Missouri

The Therapist's Notebook for Families

Solution-Oriented Exercises
for Working with Parents, Children,
and Adolescents

HAWORTH Practical Practice in Mental Health
Lorna L. Hecker, PhD
Senior Editor

101 Interventions in Family Therapy edited by Thorana S. Nelson and Terry S. Trepper

101 More Interventions in Family Therapy edited by Thorana S. Nelson and Terry S. Trepper

The Practical Practice of Marriage and Family Therapy: Things My Training Supervisor Never Told Me by Mark Odell and Charles E. Campbell

The Therapist's Notebook for Families: Solution-Oriented Exercises for Working with Parents, Children, and Adolescents by Bob Bertolino and Gary Schultheis

The Therapist's Notebook for Children and Adolescents: Homework, Handouts, and Activities for Use in Psychotherapy edited by Catherine Ford Sori and Lorna L. Hecker

The Therapist's Notebook for Lesbian, Gay, and Bisexual Clients: Homework, Handouts, and Activities for Use in Psychotherapy by Joy S. Whitman and Cynthia J. Boyd

The Therapist's Notebook for Families

Solution-Oriented Exercises for Working with Parents, Children, and Adolescents

Bob Bertolino, PhD
Gary Schultheis, MA

The Haworth Clinical Practice Press
An Imprint of The Haworth Press, Inc.
New York • London • Oxford

Published by

The Haworth Clinical Practice Press, an imprint of The Haworth Press, Inc., 10 Alice Street, Binghamton, NY 13904-1580.

Cover design by Jennifer M. Gaska.

Library of Congress Cataloging-in-Publication Data

Bertolino, Bob, 1965-
  The therapist's notebook for families : solution-oriented exercises for working with parents, children, and adolescents / Robert Bertolino, Gary Schultheis.
      p.   cm.
  Includes bibliographical references and index.
  ISBN 0-7890-1244-8 (soft)
  1. Family psychotherapy. 2. Child psychotherapy. 3. Adolescent psychotherapy. 4. Solution-focused therapy. I. Schultheis, Gary M. II. Title.

RC488.5 .B485 2002
616.89'156—dc21

2002069090

CONTENTS

PART IV: CHANGING ASPECTS OF CONTEXT

Acknowledgments

From Bob: To my wife Christine, and my daughter Morgan, all my love to you for your unconditional love and support. Thanks to Gary for his dedication and persistence with this book, for his humor, and for traveling long distances to work with me! To Bill and Steffanie O'Hanlon, thank you for your ongoing support and friendship. Thanks to my colleagues, supervisees, and students at Youth In Need, Inc., St. Louis University, and Maryville University.

From Gary: Thanks, first, to Bob for all his hard work on this project and for making it happen. Thanks also to Bill O'Hanlon for sharing his knowledge and experience over the years in a way that has been so helpful to me.

From the both of us: Thank you to the staff at The Haworth Press for seeing this book as an important contribution to the field. A special thank you to Lorna Hecker for sharing our enthusiasm and vision.

ABOUT THE AUTHORS

Bob Bertolino, PhD, is both Senior Director of Clinical Training and Clinical Director of Early Childhood Programs at Youth In Need, Inc., in St. Charles, Missouri. He is also the founder of Therapeutic Collaborations Consultation and Training, a training associate at the Institute for the Study of Therapeutic Change, and an assistant adjunct professor in the departments of counseling/family therapy and social work at St. Louis University, behavior studies at the University of Missouri–St. Louis, and rehabilitation counseling at Maryville University. Dr. Bertolino has authored or co-authored seven books, including *Therapy with Troubled Teenagers: Rewriting Young Lives in Progress, Even from a Broken Web: Brief, Respectful Solution-Oriented Therapy for Sexual Abuse and Trauma, The Residential Youth Care Worker in Action: A Collaborative, Competency-Based Approach,* and *Collaborative, Competency-Based Counseling and Therapy.* He teaches workshops nationally and internationally on collaborative, competency-based approaches to psychotherapy and clinical hypnosis. Dr. Bertolino is licensed as a marital and family therapist, professional counselor, and clinical social worker in the state of Missouri and is a National Certified Counselor.

Gary Schultheis, MA, is a psychotherapist in Evansville, Indiana. He holds a Master of Arts in Counseling from Sonoma State University. Gary has completed a two-year training program in Marriage and Family Therapy at the Menninger Clinic in St. Louis, Missouri, and has worked in the fields of probation, parole, and developmental disabilities, as well as clinical social work. He is the author of *Brief Therapy Homework Assignments,* and co-author of *Brief Couples Therapy Homework Assignments* and a computerized training program titled *Brief Therapy Coach.* In addition to counseling, Gary enjoys gardening and lampworking glass.

Introduction

Health maintenance organizations (HMOs), third-party payers, federal, state, local, and other funding sources require that mental health practitioners be accountable for creating a clear focus on goals, producing positive results, and keeping therapy relatively brief. We view this as an excellent invitation to become more accountable in the field of mental health. To do this, mental health practitioners have had to answer the following question: What works in therapy?

Despite the fact that clinicians have in excess of 250 models from which to choose, forty years of psychotherapy-outcome research has demonstrated that while most models affect change, no one approach is significantly more effective than another (Doherty and Simmons, 1995, 1996; Lambert and Bergin, 1994; Lambert, Shapiro, and Bergin, 1986; Smith, Glass, and Miller, 1980). In contrast, researchers Lambert (1992), Miller, Duncan, and Hubble (1997), Duncan and Miller (2000), and Hubble, Duncan, and Miller (1999), found that when positive change does occur in therapy, there are consistent, common factors that account for that change *regardless of the practitioner's theory.* These common factors reflect the following premises:

- Treatment should be client-informed and accommodate clients' views of the therapeutic relationship, counseling processes, goals, and tasks to accomplish those goals.
- Treatment should be change-focused as opposed to focusing on finding causes or explanations for problems except when this focus does not fit with the client.
- Emphasis should be on clients' strengths, abilities, and resources as opposed to deficits and pathology.
- Treatment should be future-oriented.
- The therapeutic relationship is paramount.
- Counselors' attitudes weigh heavily on therapeutic outcome. A focus on possibilities is essential.
- Clients should be treated as human beings, and not "depersonalized" with labels.
- Successful therapy has less to do with technique (to which counselors often attribute positive change) and more to do with client factors and the therapeutic relationship.
- Techniques are enhanced when they fit with clients' belief systems and ideas about how change will occur.

These research-supported premises form the heart and soul of a *solution-oriented* approach to therapy. To illustrate a solution-orientation and to delineate the differences between it and traditional therapeutic approaches, we offer the following diagram:

Traditional Therapy Approaches		*Solution-Oriented Therapy*
Search for impairments/deficits	→	Search for competencies/abilities
Focus is on discovering pathology	→	Focus is on promoting health/well-being
Belief is people are bad, have hidden agendas, and are resistant	→	Belief is people have good intentions, are cooperative

Focus is on the therapist finding and administering cures	→	Focus is on creating small changes that lead to bigger ones
The therapist is the "expert"	→	Therapy is collaborative—both the therapist and clients have expertise
Focus is on the past/past events	→	Focus is on the present and future
Therapists emphasize expression of emotion as necessary for change	→	Therapists validate felt experience
Therapists diagnose stuckness	→	Therapists are change-oriented
Emphasis is on finding identity and personality problems	→	Emphasis is on action and process descriptions

Solution-oriented therapy focuses on helping parents, children, and adolescents, and those associated with them to feel acknowledged, validated, and understood while simultaneously employing a collaborative process to help such persons to make changes in their lives (Bertolino, 1999; Bertolino and O'Hanlon, 2002; Bertolino and Thompson, 1999; O'Hanlon and Bertolino, 1998; O'Hanlon and Weiner-Davis, 1989). Because emphasis is on change, solution-oriented therapists tend to be active in facilitating the change process. One way of doing this is to use exercises that identify, amplify, and promote change processes. This premise has led to the creation of this manual.

THE PURPOSE OF THIS BOOK

This book was created to help mental health professionals facilitate the process of change with their clients by offering flexible, easy-to-use exercises. The exercises offered here are both for therapists *and* parents, children, adolescents, and families. The therapist-oriented exercises can be completed alone or with clients. The client-oriented exercises can be used in office-based and home-based settings or can be given to clients to complete on their own. Although we offer a solution-oriented foundation, these tools are designed to be compatible with mental health professionals' withstanding traditions and can easily be adapted to therapeutic processes. Our intention is to invite clinicians to focus on finding and using what works in therapy that is both respectful and effective in the eyes of clients.

A number of these exercises are designed for use with parents. Occasionally, a parent will wonder, "Why do I have to change when my son or daughter is the one with the problem?" There are a number of ways to respond. One possibility is to explain that we are looking for something to change and we have found that the person who is most upset by the problem is the one most likely to be willing to put forth an effort. In addition, many of the changes suggested are designed to give parents more influence in a situation in which they feel they have none.

We want to emphasize that we don't work under the assumption that clever exercises make effective therapy. Certainly, there have been a great number of therapists who have worked very effectively without ever using exercises as a tool. However, we see exercises as another means for the therapist to include those common factors that do make a difference. A good exercise will show the client that the therapist understands him or her, accepts his or her goals, and offers hope, among other things.

THE FORMAT OF THIS BOOK

This book is divided into five main sections. Each section offers specific activities that mental health professionals can use at various points in the therapeutic encounter. Part I helps clinicians to work with parents, children, adolescents, and others involved in the therapeutic process to use language that promotes change, define clear goals and preferred outcomes, and identify signs that may indicate change in the direction of those goals and outcomes.

Parts II, III, and IV focus on helping mental health professionals who work with parents, children, adolescents, and others to create change in three areas around the problem including:

- The *viewing* of the problem—This includes what clients are paying attention to in the problem situation and how they are interpreting it. It also includes the identity stories that are created and lived out by adolescents and others.
- The *doing* of the problem—This involves how clients interact with one another, including how they act during the problem situation and how they talk with one another or others about the problem. This involves searching for repeating patterns and helping parents, children, adolescents, and others to change those problematic patterns.
- Aspects of *context* associated with the problem—There are two variations here. The first is the time patterns and spatial locations associated with the problem. This will be discussed mostly in the area of changing the doing of the problem. A second way of changing the context includes attending to the influences and circumstances that surround the problem. To do this we explore contributions from familial, cultural, genetic, and gender backgrounds and propensities.

Each of the exercises provided addresses change in one of these domains and focuses on doing two things: Identifying and interrupting typical problem patterns; and seeking, highlighting, and encouraging solution patterns. To further illustrate these three areas of intervention, see Figure 1.

Part V offers tools for helping mental health professionals to identify, amplify, and promote positive change. Other areas addressed include recovering from setbacks, addressing possible future roadblocks, and the use of certificates to punctuate change. We've designed this book so that the exercises can be photocopied and given to clients.

HOW TO USE THE EXERCISES IN THIS BOOK

Each exercise is formatted in the following way:

1. Therapist's Overview
   a. Purpose of Exercise
   b. Suggestions for Use
2. Exercise

You will know the purpose of the exercise, how to use it, and any helpful hints. In addition, some specific things can assist you in the use of the exercises. First, clarity is a must. As a mental health professional it's important that you have clear goals that you are working on with the adolescents and/or families. The clearer and more specific you and your clients are about the complaint(s), the more effective your exercises will be. Thus, we've organized this book so that activities and exercises are categorized into specific areas and are easy to access.

Viewing	Doing	Context
• Points of view • Attentional patterns • Interpretations • Explanations • Assumptions • Beliefs • Identity stories	• Action patterns • Interactional patterns • Language patterns • Nonverbal patterns	• Time patterns • Physical environment/spatial location • Cultural/racial background and propensities • Family/historical background and propensities • Biochemical/genetic background and propensities • Gender training and propensities • Connections to others • Spirituality
Offer new possibilities for attention. Identify and challenge views that: *Blame* *Suggest that change is impossible* *Invalidate the person* *Suggest the person has no choice about his or her actions.*	Find patterns of action and interaction that are part of the problem and repeat. Suggest disrupting the problematic patterns or find and use solution patterns.	Identify unhelpful and helpful aspects of the context, then suggest shifts in the context around the problem (e.g., changes in biochemistry, time, space, cultural habits and influences, etc.). Use these areas to normalize (and therefore value and validate) as well as to find the problem and solution patterns in any or all of the contextual patterns.

FIGURE 1. Areas for Intervention with Adolescents and Families (*Source:* © 1996 Bill O'Hanlon) (*Note:* If you observe an item in the top row, then consider interventions from the box below it.)

Next, the use of an exercise is highly contingent on the therapeutic relationship. For example, if we offer an exercise and a parent does not believe in going home and trying it, then we would shift our approach. This is not about giving directives to unwilling clients. We are committed to hearing the voices of parents, adolescents, and family members and finding out what they feel won't work, might work, or is worthy of a try. With that said, be sure to notice the reactions of your clients when you discuss a possible exercise. If they're not interested then move on to something else.

We've also found that attending to clients' stages of change can be helpful in determining which exercises provide the best fit. Prochaska and colleagues studied people who are self-changers and those who have attended psychotherapy (Prochaska, 1995, 1999; Prochaska, DiClemente, and Norcross, 1992; Prochaska, Norcross, and DiClemente, 1994). Their research identified six stages of change and that people tend to move through stages of change in one of two ways. Some will advance in a linear fashion, passing through one stage after another. More often, people will go a second route. They will progress, relapse, progress, relapse, and cycle through the stages in a three steps forward, two steps backward process. The stages of change are as follows.

Just a brief word before you begin . . .

Using this book of exercises is going to involve some creativeness on your part. For example, although a particular exercise may have been created with parents in mind, it can be modified and changed for use with children, adolescents, and other clientele as well. So, please be sure to think "out of the box" (and you may want to start with the exercise by that name if you want to get the creative juices flowing) and challenge yourself to improve on these exercises. Your clients can only benefit!

PART I:
GETTING CLEAR ON THE CHANGE YOU WANT

1

Utilizing Collaboration Keys

THERAPIST'S OVERVIEW

Purpose of Exercise

All mental health professionals carry theories regarding the most effective arrangements for meeting with clients. Unfortunately, therapists' perceptions do not always match clients' ideas about how change will come about. However, it is clear that positive therapeutic outcome is promoted when clinicians understand and utilize their clients' ideas about how to approach therapy sessions. This is particularly important in family therapy because each person will have different ideas and all must feel included if they are to invest energy in creating solutions.

The purpose of this exercise is to help clinicians learn clients' preferences about how therapy should proceed. Client preferences provide the basis or keys for collaboration.

Suggestions for Use

1. Clinicians ought to consider utilizing Collaboration Keys during their initial phone conversations with clients, when setting appointments, and when talking with clients about their ideas and preferences regarding how treatment should proceed.
2. This exercise is designed to be completed by the therapist with clients and can be retained for reference.
3. It's important that as a clinician you set aside your theoretical biases in favor of learning clients' ideas about change. Learning clients' theories is essential in working toward positive change.
4. Even though it's important to collaborate with clients to learn about their preferences, there are times when therapists will need to dismiss or separate clients or meet in arrangements that protect them.
5. Remember that children are often unwilling participants who won't participate until they know that their views will be respected.
6. You may want to complete a copy of this exercise for each family member.

EXERCISE

The two parts of this exercise will help you learn clients' ideas about how they would like to approach their concerns and problems.

Client Name:_____   Date Completed:_____

Part 1

For the first part of this exercise, we want to learn clients' preferences regarding who they think ought to attend therapy sessions. This will help to facilitate the therapeutic relationship and assist in learning about how they believe change will come about.

To complete this part, ask clients the following questions and write their answers in the spaces provided. You may also choose to give clients this or another sheet of paper with these questions on it and ask them to write down their answers.

Who do you think should attend therapy sessions?

_____

_____

_____

Why?

_____

_____

_____

How do you think this person will help in resolving your concern? (Ask this about each person that is named by the client or person making the appointment.)

_____

_____

_____

Part 2

In this second part, we want to learn clients' ideas regarding how to meet in therapy sessions. That is, should everyone be seen together? Separate? In a combination of several formats? Once again, this will assist you in finding out from clients their ideas about how concerns and problems ought to be approached. It's important to note that clients may change their minds or develop new perspectives between sessions. Therefore, it's crucial that clinicians ask clients about their preferences on a regular basis, not just before or during the initial session. In addition, when gaining multiple perspectives, it's important to acknowledge each view and negotiate a way of working that is acceptable to each person who is present.

To complete this part, ask clients the following questions and put their answers in the spaces provided. You may also choose to give clients this or another sheet of paper with these questions on it and ask them to write down their answers.

What ideas do you have about how we should meet?

_____

_____

_____

Where did the idea come from to meet in that way?

_____

_____

_____

How do you think that arrangement might help with the concern(s) that you've come here for?

_____

_____

_____

2

Exploring Clients' Relational Preferences

THERAPIST'S OVERVIEW

Purpose of Exercise

When clients seek assistance with their concerns and problems they often enter therapy with ideas about how the practitioner can be most helpful with them. These ideas can go unnoticed if the clinician does not inquire about them. This is because many clients will not speak up about their concerns regarding therapeutic processes unless they are asked. In family sessions, a dominant voice often emerges and those who feel less included, vulnerable, or otherwise uncomfortable may be inclined to remain silent. It is important for all views to be included in any solution. Therefore, this exercise assists mental health professionals in exploring clients' ideas about how treatment ought to proceed and how the therapeutic relationship can best facilitate positive change processes.

Suggestions for Use

1. This exercise is to be completed by the therapist. You may want to complete one for each family member.
2. This exercise can be used early in therapy to learn clients' ideas about how they would like the clinician to be in relationship with them. It can also be used at any point when the therapist has any uncertainty regarding his or her effectiveness and/or approach.
3. This exercise can be done using the worksheet that is provided or the clinician can simply ask the questions as a way of learning clients' relational preferences.
4. Don't be surprised if children are unprepared, suspicious, or threatened when you ask their opinions. Remember that simply asking for their opinions implies that you value them. There may be many reasons that they may not be able to respond to these questions. You can let them know that they may express their opinions any time in the future.

EXERCISE

It's important to learn clients' perceptions of the therapeutic relationship, including their ideas regarding the role of therapists in facilitating change. Psychotherapy outcome research suggests that therapists who are able to match clients' expectations of the therapeutic relationship increase the likelihood of successful outcome. In addition, a strong therapeutic relationship in the eyes of clients can create a foundation that facilitates intervention.

1. To learn clients' ideas about the therapeutic relationship in initial sessions, consider the following questions. In doing this, identify which ones would best fit with your way of working with clients.

- What ideas do you have about how I can be helpful to you?
- In what ways do you see me as being helpful to you in reaching your goals?
- What are the things that you want to be sure that we talk about?
- How will you know that I have been helpful to you?
- What ideas do you have about how therapists can be helpful with clients?
- What qualities do you look for in a therapist?

Next, write down the questions you have chosen in the spaces provided along with your clients' responses. Then, try out the questions that you've chosen during your interactions with your clients. You may also choose to write down a couple of these questions and give them to clients to complete as an exercise.

Question: _____

Response: _____

_____

_____

Question: _____

Response: _____

_____

_____

Question: _____

Response: _____

_____

_____

The answers to these questions can help clinicians learn from clients how they view the therapeutic relationship and how helpers can facilitate change processes in ways that are consistent with clients' perceptions.

2. To learn about clients' perceptions of the therapeutic relationship after there has been some interaction, consider the following questions. As with the previous questions, identify the ones that best fit your way of working with clients.

- Do you feel/think we're talking about what you want to talk about?
- Are we moving in a direction that seems right for you?
- How has the conversation we've been having been helpful?
- What have I been doing that has been helpful or unhelpful with you?
- Are there other things that you feel/think we should be discussing instead?
- Is there anything I should be doing differently?

Next, try out the questions that you've chosen during your interactions with your clients. Write down the questions you have chosen in the spaces provided along with your clients' responses. You may also choose to write down a couple of these questions and give them to clients to complete as an exercise.

Question: _____

Response: _____

_____

_____

Question: _____

Response: _____

_____

_____

Question: _____

Response: _____

_____

_____

Research suggests that if clinicians do not ask clients about their perceptions of the therapeutic relationship, few will voluntarily offer them. However, not knowing clients' thoughts and ideas can negatively affect outcome. Therefore, clients' answers to the questions in Parts 1 and 2 can help mental health professionals to learn what is working and what is not working in the therapeutic relationship. Based on this information, clinicians can do more of what works and do away with what does not—making any necessary changes and adjustments along the way.

3. In the spaces provided, write down questions that you have found helpful in learning about clients' relational preferences. These can be questions that were listed in this exercise or new questions that you developed. In the future, refer back to these questions if you become stuck with clients.

_____

_____

_____

_____

The Language of Change:
Using Action-Talk

THERAPIST'S OVERVIEW

Purpose of Exercise

The words we use to describe what is going on in families are very important when it comes to creating the desired change. The clearer we are on what we want to see change, the more ideas we will be able to generate. In contrast, our vagueness can lead us in a multitude of unhelpful directions.

The purpose of this exercise is to help parents use "action-talk" to describe the behaviors that are problematic. Action-talk allows clinicians, parents, adolescents, and others to gain a clear, behavioral description of the complaint. We refer to this as the "doing" of the problem. This question asks, "When your son/daughter misbehaves, what does he or she do?"

This exercise can be used at any point in therapy when clients are using vague, nondescriptive words such as misbehavior, disobedient, out-of-control, hyperactive, and so on. It can also be helpful to clinicians in those instances when there is a lack of clarity regarding the focus of therapy.

Suggestions for Use

1. The following two exercises are designed to be completed by clients. The first is appropriate for adults, the second, for teens or older children.
2. Give examples of changing vague, nondescriptive translations of problems into clear, observable, behavioral descriptions by using action-talk.
3. Explain or demonstrate how vague descriptions of concerns and complaints can lead to unhelpful or misguided attempts at solving problems and finding solutions.
4. Once they have used action-talk, ask clients what new ideas they might have about how to deal with the complaint.

EXERCISE

To avoid using vague, nondescriptive language when talking about the problems we're facing with adolescents (e.g., acting out, throwing tantrums, misbehaving, etc.) we'll use "action-talk." Action-talk helps us to determine the "doing" of the problem. That is, what does your son or daughter *do* when he or she is misbehaving/acting out/out-of-control, etc.? Let's see how we can use action-talk to move from vague problem descriptions:

Vague problem description	Action-talk questions	Action-talk description
My son has a problem with his anger.	→ What has your son done that tells you that he's got a problem with his anger?	→ He's hit me and broken things in the house.
He loses control.	→ When he loses control what do you see him doing?	→ He throws things and calls me bad names.
She's self-destructive.	→ What does she do during those times that you feel she's being self-destructive?	→ She cuts on her arms with glass or sharp objects.

Now it's your turn. In the left column in the following list are a few examples of vague problem descriptions. Your goal is to find some possible endings to each sentence in the right column by using action-talk.

Vague problem description		Action-talk description
My daughter is irresponsible.	→	When my daughter is behaving irresponsibly she _____ _____
My son is out of control.	→	When my son is out of control he _____ _____ _____
My daughter has poor social skills.	→	When my daughter is having trouble socially she _____ _____
My son is hyperactive.	→	When my son is acting hyperactive he _____ _____ _____

Action-talk allows us to target specific behaviors as opposed to trying to figure out what will work best with vague words such as ADHD, oppositional, defiant, and so on. When you are clear about what you want to see change, then you can focus very specifically on changing behaviors as opposed to diagnoses or characterizations.

To gain clarity regarding the concerns you're having with your adolescent, use the left column as follows to list those concerns. Then, in the right column, if necessary, use action-talk to get a clearer picture of your complaint.

Problem description	Action-talk description (if not clear in first column)
1. _____	→1. _____
_____	_____
_____	_____

2. _____→2. _____

_____   _____

_____   _____

3. _____→3. _____

_____   _____

_____   _____

4. _____→4. _____

_____   _____

_____   _____

5. _____→5. _____

_____   _____

_____   _____

EXERCISE

To avoid using vague, nondescriptive language when talking about the problems we're facing (e.g., being overprotective, being nosey, etc.) we'll use "action-talk." Action-talk helps us to determine the "doing" of the problem. That is, what does your parent(s) do when he or she is nosey or overprotective? Let's see how we can use action-talk to move from vague problem descriptions:

Vague problem description	Action-talk questions	Action-talk description
My parents don't trust me.	→ What have your parents done that tells you they don't trust you?	→ Mom searched my room.
They are overprotective.	→ What do they do that you call overprotective?	→ They make me come home at 11 p.m. on weekends.
They embarrass me in front of my friends.	→ What have they done that embarrassed you?	→ Dad lectured me about cleaning my room in front of my girlfriend.

Now it's your turn. In the following list, in the left column, are a few examples of vague problem descriptions. Your goal is to find some possible endings to each sentence in the right column by using action-talk.

Vague problem description		Action-talk description
My parents are bossy.	→	When my parents are bossy they _____ _____ _____
My parents disrespect me.	→	When my parents "dis" me they _____ _____ _____
My parents don't understand.	→	My parents show that they don't understand me when they _____ _____ _____
My parents expect too much of me.	→	My parents expect too much when they _____ _____ _____

Action-talk allows us to target specific behaviors as opposed to trying to figure out what will work best with vague words such as disrespect, don't understand, and so on. When you are clear about what you want to see change, then you can focus very specifically on changing behaviors as opposed to changing personalities.

To gain clarity regarding the issues you're having with your parents, use the left column to list those concerns. Then, in the right column, if necessary, use action-talk to get a clearer picture of your complaint.

Problem description   **Action-talk description (if not clear in first column)**

1. _____ →1. _____

_____   _____

_____   _____

2. _____ →2. _____

_____   _____

_____   _____

3. _____ →3. _____

_____   _____

_____   _____

4. _____ →4. _____

_____   _____

_____   _____

5. _____ → 5. _____

_____   _____

_____   _____

Defining the Problem:
Determining What Needs to Change

THERAPIST'S OVERVIEW

Purpose of Exercise

When parents, adolescents, and those involved with adolescents are unclear about what they want to change, attempts at finding solutions may be misguided. This can lead to frustration on the part of clients when things don't seem to be improving. In addition, clinicians can become frustrated, as they are unsure of the goals of therapy. This can also lead to the use of interventions that do not target specific problems, only vague descriptions of problems.

The purpose of this exercise is to clearly define what needs to change (the goals of therapy) and prioritize problems. In this way, both clients and clinicians can be clear about what is the focus of therapy. This exercise can be used at the start of therapy when goals are being established, or at any juncture when the goal or goals need to be modified or changed altogether.

Note: This activity involves the use of "action-talk." To learn about this, please refer to the activity, "The Language of Change: Using Action-Talk."

Suggestions for Use

1. Talk with clients about how to use "action-talk" so that they can begin to change their descriptions of problems into clear, behavioral, and observable ones.
2. Help clients to determine what they want as opposed to what they don't want. For example, if a parent says that he or she doesn't want his or her son to run away, inquire as to what the parent would like to see the youth doing instead. That is, what are the behaviors that the parent would like to have happen?
3. Some clients need assistance in determining which goals ought to take precedence. Help them to decide what needs to change first, second, and so on. We frequently remind clients that oftentimes only a small change is necessary. Little changes can lead to further changes much like a snowball gaining momentum as it rolls down a hill.
4. Since it is common to have multiple goals in therapy, keep in mind that there may be different goals set by the adolescent, parents, and others involved. In such cases, have each person complete the exercise on his or her own. Also bear in mind that goals need to be "doable." That is, they need to be realistic, attainable, ethical, and legal. For example, it may not be realistic for an adolescent to *never* talk back to his or her parents. Rather, a realistic goal might be that 75 percent of the time, instead of talking back, an adolescent who becomes upset will choose behaviors that are acceptable to his or her parent(s). Another possibility might be that an adolescent can disagree with his or her parents as long as he or she uses respectful language that is not profanity-laced. Unrealistic and unattainable goals can lead to a sense of failure. An example of an unethical or illegal goal might be for an adolescent to steal less or for a parent to be less abusive. Stealing and abuse are never okay and thus, such goals should not be established.

EXERCISE

What things would you like to see change with your family, or in your life?

1. _____

2. _____

3. _____

4. _____

5. _____

Next, if you haven't already done so, translate each of the different things that you would like to see change into "action-talk." Action-talk means that we take our vague descriptions of our concerns and change them into clear, behavioral ones. This allows us to understand the "doing" of the problem. Remember to specify what you want to have happen instead of the problematic behavior(s).

Example of vague description: "I want my son to stop being so out of control" or "I want my parents to stop treating me like a baby."

Translation to action-talk description: "I want my son to talk with me, someone else, or walk away when he becomes angry" or "I want my parents to be respectful of me in front of my friends by waiting until we are alone to discuss their concerns with me."

1. _____

2. _____

3. _____

4. _____

5. _____

Now, list in order the action-based descriptions of things that you would like to see change. All of your concerns are important but it's important to start with the ones that you want to see change first. These will represent the goals of therapy.

1. _____

2. _____

3. _____

4. _____

5. _____

Clarifying Preferred Outcomes:
How Will We Know When Things Are Better?

THERAPIST'S OVERVIEW

Purpose of Exercise

When clients have defined what it is that they want to change, it's important to help them to determine how they will know when they've achieved those goals or preferred outcomes. Ambiguity regarding therapy goals can lead to uncertainty about when success has been achieved and therapy can be ended.

The purpose of this exercise is to go beyond defining what clients want to finding out how they will know when that change has been achieved. In this way, both clients and clinicians can be clear about what will constitute a successful outcome. This type of exercise is often helpful for teens who need clarity regarding what will indicate change to others.

This exercise can be used at the start of therapy, in conjunction with establishing goals. It can also be used at any juncture when goals have been modified or changed altogether.

Note: This activity involves the use of "action-talk." To learn about this, please refer to the activity, "The Language of Change: Using Action-Talk." This activity also is used in conjunction with "Defining the Problem: Determining What Needs to Change."

Suggestions for Use

1. This exercise is written for adults. Exercises more appropriate for teens follow.
2. Talk with clients about how to use "action-talk" so that they can begin to change their descriptions of outcomes into clear, behavioral, and observable ones.
3. Help clients to define outcomes that are realistic and attainable.
4. Because clients' ideas about how change will look will vary, preferred outcomes should incorporate each person's views of the future.

EXERCISE

There is an old saying, "If you don't know where you're going you'll probably end up somewhere else." If you were going on a vacation to a far-away destination, would you just choose a flight to anywhere or jump in the car and start driving and hope that you arrive at your destination? Probably not. This exercise will help you to determine your preferred destination so that you will know when the outcome you are seeking has been achieved.

To complete this exercise, refer back to the goals that you established during the exercise, "Defining the Problem: Determining What Needs to Change." Next, write those goals down in the spaces provided.

Example: I would like my daughter to handle her anger better in the future by talking to me or leaving a volatile situation until she has calmed down.

1. _____

2. _____

3. _____

4. _____

5. _____

Next, ask yourself, "How will I know when the problem I'm/we're facing is no longer a problem?" Then, for each of the goals previously listed, write down a corresponding preferred outcome. Be as specific as possible and use action-talk means when creating these outcomes.

Example: I will know that my daughter is handling her anger better when she is able to talk to me or walk away from volatile situations eight out of ten times.

1. _____

2. _____

3. _____

4. _____

5. _____

6

The Crystal Ball

THERAPIST'S OVERVIEW

Purpose of Exercise

The Crystal Ball is one of many creative ways of helping adolescents create visions of their preferred futures—the kinds of futures where things work out for them. Once these visions of the future have been created, mental health professionals and others can work with adolescents to identify steps that will help them to reach those preferred futures.

The purpose of this exercise is to help adolescents identify how they will know when things are better in their lives. In this way, both clients and clinicians can be clear about what will constitute a successful outcome. This type of exercise is often helpful for teens who fear that therapy may be interminable. Frequently, they become more motivated in therapy when they realize that it will end when the goals are reached.

This exercise can be used at the start of therapy, in conjunction with establishing goals. It can also be used at any juncture when goals have been modified or changed altogether.

Note: This activity involves the use of "action-talk." To learn about this, please refer to the activity, "The Language of Change: Using Action-Talk."

Suggestions for Use

1. Talk with adolescents about how to use "action-talk" so that they can begin to change their descriptions of preferred futures and outcomes into clear, behavioral, and observable ones.
2. Help adolescents to define preferred futures and outcomes that are realistic and attainable.
3. Allow adolescents to be creative in modifying this exercise as they see fit.

EXERCISE

This exercise will help you to describe what it is that you want for yourself in the future. To complete this exercise, consider the following:

Imagine that there is a crystal ball sitting in front of you. This is a special kind of crystal ball. It's one that helps you to see yourself in the future. Now peer into the crystal ball. Notice that you can see the kind of future that you want for yourself—the kind of future where things work out for you.

Now, in the crystal ball that has been provided, write down what you see happening in your future. What are you doing? How did you solve your problem(s)? What did you do? Did anyone help you? What did that person do to help you?

Next, in the spaces provided, write down five things that you could do right now or in the next few days, weeks, or months to begin to move toward the future that you've envisioned, to make it a reality.

1. _____

2. _____

3. _____

4. _____

5. _____

7

The Time Machine

THERAPIST'S OVERVIEW

Purpose of Exercise

The Time Machine is one of many creative ways to help adolescents create visions of their preferred futures—the kinds of futures where things work out for them. Once these visions of the future have been created, mental health professionals and others can work with adolescents to identify steps that will help them to reach those preferred futures.

The purpose of this exercise is to help adolescents identify how they will know when things are better in their lives. In this way, both clients and clinicians can be clear about what will constitute a successful outcome.

This type of exercise is often helpful for teens who fear that therapy may never end. Frequently, they become more motivated in therapy when they realize that it will end when the goals are reached. This exercise can be used at the start of therapy, in conjunction with establishing goals. It can also be used at any juncture when goals have been modified or changed altogether.

Note: This activity involves the use of "action-talk." To learn about this, please refer to the activity, "The Language of Change: Using Action-Talk."

Suggestions for Use

1. Talk with adolescents about how to use "action-talk" so they can begin to change their descriptions of preferred futures and outcomes into clear, behavioral, and observable ones.
2. Help adolescents define preferred futures and outcomes that are realistic and attainable.
3. Allow adolescents to be creative in modifying this exercise as they see fit.
4. Consider ending therapy as a motivator.

EXERCISE

This exercise will help you to describe what it is that you want for yourself in the future. It requires a little imagination on your part. Are you ready?

To complete this exercise, consider the following:

Imagine that there is a time machine sitting in the room with you. This time machine can propel you into the future to a time when things are going the way you'd like.

Now, in the box that has been provided, write down what you see happening in your future. What are you doing? How did you solve your problem(s)? What did you do? Did anyone help you? What did that person do to help you?

Next, in the spaces that follow, write down five things that you could do right now or in the next few days, weeks, or months to begin to move toward the future that you've envisioned and to make it a reality.

1. _____

2. _____

3. _____

4. _____

5. _____

8

Defining In-Between Change:
How Will I Know When We're Making Progress?

THERAPIST'S OVERVIEW

Purpose of Exercise

When clients have defined what it is that they want to change and the outcomes they prefer, it's important to help them determine how they will know they are making progress toward established goals and outcomes. By identifying "in-between" changes, clients can notice that they are making progress, therefore promoting hope and facilitating further change. This is particularly important because some clients will become frustrated or anxious, and perhaps give up if they do not have the sense that they are making progress toward their goals. Adolescents are notoriously impatient when they want change. In addition, actions that further progress toward goals are the best guide in deciding what further action is needed.

The purpose of this exercise is to work with clients to identify "signs" that they are beginning to get the upper hand and are making progress with the problems they have outlined. This exercise can be used at the start of therapy in conjunction with establishing goals and preferred outcomes. It can also be used at any juncture when goals and outcomes have been modified or changed altogether.

Note: This activity involves the use of "action-talk." To learn about this, please refer to the activity, "The Language of Change: Using Action-Talk." This activity also is used in conjunction with "Defining the Problem: Determining What Needs to Change" and "Clarifying Outcomes: How Will We Know When Things Are Better?"

Suggestions for Use

1. Talk with clients about how to use "action-talk" so that they can begin to change their descriptions of in-between changes into clear, behavioral, and observable ones.
2. Help clients to define in-between changes that are realistic and attainable.
3. Because clients' ideas about how change will look will vary, in-between changes should incorporate each person's views of the future.
4. Acknowledge helpful actions that teens, in particular, take as the result of this exercise, or have taken even before therapy began.

EXERCISE

This exercise will help you identify indicators of change and how much progress you are making toward the goals and preferred outcomes that you established. In this way, you will have a clear idea of what to look for as you focus on working toward the changes you are seeking.

To complete this exercise, refer back to the outcomes that you established during the exercise, "Clarifying Preferred Outcomes: How Will We Know When Things Are Better?" Next, write those preferred outcomes in the spaces provided.

Example: We want homework to be completed each weeknight following dinner.

1. _____

2. _____

3. _____

4. _____

5. _____

Next, ask yourself, "How will I/we know when I/we are making progress with the problem(s) I'm/we're facing?" Then, for each of the preferred outcomes previously listed, write down at least two "signs" that will indicate that progress is being made. Be as specific as possible and use action-talk means when creating these signs or indicators of change.

Example:

Preferred Outcome: We want homework to be completed each weeknight following dinner.

Signs:

All books necessary for homework will be brought home from school.
Homework will begin following dinner with no more than two reminders.
Teen will ask for help on homework if needed.

Preferred Outcome #1

_____

Signs: _____

_____

Preferred Outcome #2

_____

Signs: _____

_____

Preferred Outcome #3

_____

Signs: _____

_____

Preferred Outcome #4

_____

Signs: _____

_____

Preferred Outcome #5

_____

Signs: _____

_____

9

Using Video-Talk

THERAPIST'S OVERVIEW

Purpose of Exercise

This exercise offers an alternative way of helping parents, children, adolescents, and family members to construct goals, preferred outcomes, and to identify in-between changes. This can help clients numerically measure and chart the changes that they are seeking.

The purpose of this exercise is to provide clients with an alternative for monitoring progress from the establishment of goals and preferred outcomes through the identification of smaller changes that signify progress toward preferred outcomes. This exercise can be used at the start of therapy or when new goals have been created.

Note: This activity involves the use of "action-talk." To learn about this, please refer to the exercise, "The Language of Change: Using Action-Talk." This activity may also be used concurrently with "Defining the Problem: Determining What Needs to Change," "Clarifying Preferred Outcomes," and "Defining In-Between Change."

Suggestions for Use

1. Talk with clients about how to use "action-talk" so that they can begin to change their descriptions of goals, preferred outcomes, and indicators of in-between change into clear, behavioral, and observable ones.
2. Consider setting up the exercise by saying something like, "If we had a video camera and we taped your family, what would we see happening? Now, let's take this a step further and apply this to the problem(s) you've been facing.
3. Be sure that the goals, preferred outcomes, and in-between changes that are established are realistic, specific, and observable.

EXERCISE

This exercise will help you to clarify what it is that you would like to see change, how you will know when you've achieved those changes, and what will constitute progress toward those changes.

To complete this exercise, imagine that you had a video camera and were able to tape your family and perhaps others, as the problem happened. Then, imagine that the videotape was put into a VCR and played. What would be seen on that tape that would indicate that there was a problem? What would each person be doing? Who else would be present? What would make it clear that it was a problem?

In the space provided, please answer the questions. Be sure to use action-talk. Action-talk means that we take vague descriptions of our concerns and change them into clear, behavioral ones. This allows us to understand the "doing" of the problem.

_____

_____

_____

_____

_____

_____

_____

_____

Next, imagine that a video camera was used to tape your family in the future when the problem was no longer a problem and things were going more the way you'd like. When that tape was played in a VCR, what would be seen on it that would indicate that things were better? What would each person be doing? Once again, use action-talk to describe what would be seen.

_____

_____

_____

_____

_____

_____

_____

_____

For this final part, imagine that it was possible to videotape your family at the very moment when things had started to turn the corner in regard to the problem(s) you've been experiencing.

The video camera was able to capture the progress that had been made with the problem. When the videotape was played, what would be seen on that tape to indicate that the problem was beginning to fade? What would each of you be saying and doing? Remember to use action-talk to describe what would be seen.

_____

_____

_____

_____

_____

_____

_____

_____

_____

10

Scaling Goals, Preferred Outcomes, and Signs of Change

THERAPIST'S OVERVIEW

Purpose of Exercise

This exercise offers a way of helping parents, children, adolescents, and family members to quantitatively construct goals, preferred outcomes, and to identify in-between changes. This can help clients numerically measure and chart the changes that they are seeking.

The purpose of this exercise is to provide clients with an alternative for monitoring progress from the establishment of goals and preferred outcomes through the identification of smaller changes that signify progress toward preferred outcomes. This exercise can be used at the start of therapy or when new goals have been created.

Note: This exercise involves the use of "action-talk." To learn about this, please refer to the exercise, "The Language of Change: Using Action-Talk." This activity may also be used concurrently with "Defining the Problem: Determining What Needs to Change," "Clarifying Preferred Outcomes," and "Defining In-Between Change."

Suggestions for Use

1. This exercise can be completed in the therapy session or given to clients to complete at home.
2. Talk with clients about how to use "action-talk" so that they can begin to change their descriptions of goals, preferred outcomes, and indicators of in-between change into clear, behavioral, and observable ones.
3. Multiple scales may be necessary if there is a significant variance between clients' goals.
4. It's generally useful to use a scale of 1-10. In this way, clients are starting from a positive number.
5. Some clients may strive for a "10" in terms of the outcome they are seeking. A 10 represents "perfect," which will be unrealistic for most people. Therefore, it's generally helpful to remind clients that they should choose a number that will indicate that the problem(s) they sought help for is no longer a problem or that treatment has been successful.
6. When working with clients to identify in-between changes or signs of change, it's generally better to have them select small increments of change. For example, instead of suggesting that clients identify what will indicate movement from a 3 to a 6, suggest movement from a 3 to a 3 ¼ or 3 ½. This may help them to work toward smaller, more realistic changes and improve their chances of achieving success.
7. Scaling is one way to respond to a teen's complaint that "They never see the good stuff I do."

EXERCISE

Through a process of scaling, this exercise will help you to identify what it is that you want to see change, how you will know when that change has occurred, and what will indicate to you that progress is being made toward the goals and outcomes that you have outlined. To complete this exercise, please follow the directions in Parts 1 through 4.

Part 1

First, write down what it is that you would like to see change. Be sure to use action-talk. Action-talk means that we take vague descriptions of our concerns and change them into clear, behavioral ones. This allows us to understand the "doing" of the problem.

1. _____

2. _____

3. _____

4. _____

5. _____

Next, using a scale from 1-10, where 1 represents the worst that things could be regarding the problem(s) and 10 represents the best that things could be in regard to the problem(s), in the blank provided, please write down the number that best corresponds to your situation now.

Part 1 Scale Rating: _____

Part 2

In this section, you're going to determine what you would like to see happening in the future, when things are going more the way you'd like with you and/or your adolescent. To do this, ask yourself, "How will I know when the problem I'm/we're facing is no longer a problem?" or "How will I know that therapy has been successful with the problem for which I/we sought help?" Then, for each of the concerns listed in Part 1, write down a corresponding preferred outcome. It's important that you write down what you would like to see happen with you and/or your adolescent *instead* of the problem that you've been experiencing. Also, be as specific as possible and use action-talk when creating these outcomes.

1. _____

2. _____

3. _____

4. _____

5. _____

Next, using the same scale described in Part 1 of this exercise, in the blank provided, please write down the number that you feel would have to be achieved for you to feel that the problem(s) you're facing is no longer a problem, that therapy has been successful, and/or that things are better in regard to the problem(s) for which you sought help.

Part 2 Scale Rating: _____

Part 3

In this part we will work toward helping you to identify signs or indicators that the change(s) you are seeking is occurring. To do this, ask yourself, "What would indicate that things are starting to go better with the problem I'm/we're facing?" or "What will signify to me/others that things have started to turn the corner with the problem(s) for which we sought help?" Try to identify small changes first. Then, in the spaces provided, for each of the preferred outcomes you listed in Part 2, write down at least two "signs" that will indicate that progress is being made. Next, write down a number on a scale from 1-10 that would correspond with each sign of change. That is, what will the achievement of the sign or indicator represent numerically? Be as specific as possible and use action-talk means when creating these signs or indicators of change.

Preferred Outcome #1

_____

Signs: _____   Scale Rating: _____

_____   Scale Rating: _____

Preferred Outcome #2

_____

Signs: _____   Scale Rating: _____

_____   Scale Rating: _____

Preferred Outcome #3

_____

Signs: _____   Scale Rating: _____

_____   Scale Rating: _____

Preferred Outcome #4

_____

Signs: _____   Scale Rating: _____

_____   Scale Rating: _____

Preferred Outcome #5

_____

Signs: _____   Scale Rating: _____

_____   Scale Rating: _____

Part 4

In this final section, in the spaces provided, write down each of the scales that you have completed in the previous three parts.

1. *Part 1 Scale Rating* (The number that best represents where things are now with the problem I/we're facing)

_____

2. *Part 2 Scale Rating* (The number that will indicate that the problem we've been facing is no longer a problem and/or that therapy has been successful)

_____

3. *Part 3 Scale Rating* (The numbers that will indicate that we are making progress toward the outcomes I've/we've established)

_____ _____ _____ _____ _____

In the future, refer to this chart as a way of monitoring where you are in terms of making progress toward the outcomes that you've established. You can also continue to identify further signs and indicators that change is occurring and scale those as well.

11

Exploring Clients' Theories of Change

THERAPIST'S OVERVIEW

Purpose of Exercise

Traditionally, therapists have been trained in the theory of human development and problem formation. In recent years, more attention has been placed on theories that encourage change processes in therapy with less emphasis placed on the past. We think it is important to remember that clients come to us with their own experiences and ideas about what works for them. If therapists are too enamored with their own theories to the exclusion of clients' ideas, they risk losing rapport as well as missing therapeutic opportunities presented by clients.

The purpose of this exercise is to help clients express their ideas about how they may best make changes. In turn, therapists can learn what clients want and expect from therapy and how they can best match those views.

Suggestions for Use

1. This exercise could be completed in a therapy session or at home.
2. This exercise can be used early in therapy to help the therapist know how to be most helpful in addressing the client's concerns. It can also be used later on if the therapy seems to be stuck in some way and the therapist needs to know more about the client's ideas about change.
3. In subsequent sessions, through periodic "check-ins," the therapist may raise the question of whether he or she is following the client's theory of change.
4. The information received in this exercise may also be revisited to examine how the client's ideas may have expanded or changed.
5. Be prepared for a negative response to this exercise from a teen who isn't keen on being in therapy. You may want to proceed without input from a teen on this subject, and, instead, discover what works for this particular client during therapy. You can then explore this with the client. It may be information that is helpful to your client even after therapy is complete.
6. Some teens will be surprised that you are asking their opinion on how best to proceed. You may get a hostile response or simply one of confusion. Either way, it is a good opportunity to explain that the best therapy is usually a collaboration. This can often have the effect of softening hostility.

EXERCISE

Although your therapist has a lot of training, you know more about yourself. You know what hasn't worked, what has worked (to any degree), and what might work in the future. You also have preferences about how your concerns might best be approached. The more your therapist knows about you, the more helpful therapy can be.

There are two parts to this exercise. In Part 1, please take some time to think over the following questions about your past experiences with learning and change. Then, for each question, circle the answer or answers that best fit you. You may choose more than one answer for each question.

Part 1

1. *I tend to learn best . . .*
   By having something told to me over and over.
   By reading as much as I can on a subject.
   From the experiences of other people.
   By realizing rewards when I succeed.
   By making mistakes and learning from them.
   By being shown where I am wrong.
   Other (please list): _____

2. *My therapist can be of greatest assistance by . . .*
   Telling me what I should do.
   Asking questions and encouraging me to look deeper into my own ideas.
   Sharing his or her ideas.
   Suggesting reading.
   Suggesting actions for me to experiment with.
   Just listening.
   Other (please list): _____

3. *I expect change to happen . . .*
   All at once.
   Step by step.
   In increments.
   Quickly.
   Slowly.
   Not at all.
   Other (please list): _____

4. *I expect change to happen in my therapy . . .*
   By gaining insight into how I got this problem.
   Through trying new things until we find something that works.
   Other (please list): _____

5. *I think that I need to change . . .*
   Something deep in my personality.
   The way I think about or look at things.
   Some thing(s) that I do.
   Someone else.
   Other (please list): _____

Part 2

Oftentimes, people have a pretty good hunch not only about what is causing a problem, but also about how to resolve it. Here we'll explore your ideas related to these areas. To complete Part 2 of this exercise, please review the questions, and in the spaces provided, write down your responses.

1. What ideas do you have about what is causing the concern/problem(s) that you're facing?

_____

_____

_____

_____

_____

2. What ideas do you have about how change is going to happen with your concern/problem(s)?

_____

_____

_____

_____

_____

3. Given the ideas that you have about the problem you're facing, what do you think would be the first step in addressing it? _____

_____

_____

_____

_____

4. What else might you do differently as a result of the theory you've developed? _____

_____

_____

_____

_____

_____

Once you've finished, take a moment to review your responses. Consider what you have learned about yourself, the concern/problem(s) you're facing, and how you might achieve the change that you are seeking.

PART II:
CHANGING THE VIEWING OF THE PROBLEM

12

Changing Language Through Acknowledgment and Possibility

THERAPIST'S OVERVIEW

Purpose of Exercise

When parents and adolescents describe their concerns, problems, and situations they will often use descriptions that close down the possibilities for change. They will use words or phrases such as "always," "nobody," "never," "all the time," etc. These descriptions imply that things cannot change and are pervasive. Many adolescents are sensitive to criticism and may hear "always" or "never" even when those words are not spoken. If a teen feels that positive behaviors are not noticed, there may be little incentive to change behaviors described as negative. If on one hand a therapist uses pure reflection with such concerns (e.g., "Things are always bad," "He'll never change," etc.) then the descriptions is in effect being reinforced. On the other hand, if a therapist takes too big a leap in challenging a parent's or adolescent's description (e.g., "Things are always bad?" "He'll never change?" etc.) then the parent or adolescent may feel invalidated and that the therapist doesn't understand the seriousness of the concern.

There are two purposes for this exercise. First, it's important that parents and adolescents feel heard and understood. Therefore, we want to use acknowledgment and reflection so that they know that we hear their concerns. However, as described, if we only reflect, they will likely remain stuck as will the clinician. To neutralize this we add a second part. As a second part, along with acknowledgment, we add the element of possibility.

Suggestions for Use

1. This exercise is mainly for therapists but can be given to clients to help them raise their level of awareness regarding the importance of language.
2. As a clinician, it's important to tune your ears to words, phrases, or descriptions that suggest impossibility (e.g., "always," "never," etc.).
3. It's important that clients aren't dramatically changed. The idea is to combine pure reflection and acknowledgment with small changes in language that suggest that there are possibilities for change.

Note: This exercise is an adjunct to "Future Talk: Acknowledgment and a Vision for the Future."

EXERCISE

If clients do not feel heard and understood they will likely close down, become angry, or let therapists know in some way that there is a problem. Still, as we listen and attend to clients, if we only reflect back their experiences many will continue to box themselves into corners by describing situations that seem hopeless, with no way out. What we want to do is add a twist to the idea of pure reflection.

There are two parts to this exercise. In Part 1, in the spaces provided, use each corresponding method of acknowledging while simultaneously offering possibilities for change. In Part 2, combine two or more of the methods offered to acknowledge and intersperse possibilities through language.

Part 1

1. Reflect back clients' responses or problem reports in the past tense.

Examples:

CLIENT: "He's always in trouble."
THERAPIST: "So *he's been* in trouble a lot."
CLIENT: "Things will never change."
THERAPIST: "*Up to this point,* things haven't changed."

Client: "She always forgets to do her homework."
Therapist: _____

Client: "Nobody ever understands me."
Therapist: _____

Client: "I never get a chance because they don't like me."
Therapist: _____

2. Take clients' general statements such as "everything," "everybody," "nobody," "always," and "never" and translate them into partial statements. This can be done by using qualifiers related to time (e.g., recently, in the last while, in the past month or so, most of the time, much of the time), intensity (e.g., a bit less, somewhat more), or partiality (e.g., a lot, some, most, many).

Examples:

CLIENT: "I get in trouble all the time."
THERAPIST: "So you get in trouble *a lot of the time.*"
CLIENT: "Nothing ever goes right for me."
THERAPIST: "*Sometimes* it seems like nothing goes right."

Client: "She's always out of control."
Therapist: _____

Client: "He never thinks about anyone but himself."
Therapist: _____

Client: "Every time I try, something goes wrong."
Therapist: _____

It's important to recognize that if clients feel like their experiences are being minimized, or if they feel pushed to move on, they will likely respond with a statement such as "Not most of the time! All the time!" If the person reacts in such a manner, then we are not getting it right. We must then move to validate further to make sure clients feel heard and understood. We can still do so while keeping an eye on possibilities. We want to let clients know that we have heard and understood their suffering, concerns, felt-experience, and points of view, without closing down the possibilities for change.

3. Translate clients' statements of truth or reality—the way they explain things for themselves—into perceptual statements or subjective realities (e.g., "It seems to you . . . ," "You've gotten the idea . . . ," etc.).

Examples:

CLIENT: "I can't do anything right."
THERAPIST: "*You've really gotten the idea* that you can't do anything right."
CLIENT: "He'll never amount to anything."
THERAPIST: "Because of what he's done, *it seems to you* that he'll never amount to anything."

Client: "Everyone hates me."
Therapist: _____

Client: "Nobody knows how hard it is to get along with her."
Therapist: _____

Client: "It's always bad in school."
Therapist: _____

Part 2

In Part 2 of this exercise, in the spaces provided, combine two or more of the methods to acknowledge clients and simultaneously offer possibilities for change.

Examples:

CLIENT: "My life is horrible and will never get any better."
THERAPIST: "You're life *has been* horrible and it really *seems to you* that it won't get any better."
CLIENT: "I'm a bad person because I'm always in trouble."
THERAPIST: "So *you've really gotten the idea* that you are bad because *you've been* in trouble."

Client: "He does whatever he wants, whenever he wants."
Therapist: _____

Client: "She's always nagging me about something and won't give up until she gets her way."
Therapist: _____

Client: "Everybody thinks I'm stupid because I have bad grades."
Therapist: _____

13

Future Talk: Acknowledgment and a Vision for the Future

THERAPIST'S OVERVIEW

Purpose of Exercise

With some clients, the language they use to describe themselves, others, and their situations seems to hold them as prisoners of the present or past with little or no sense of a future without problems, pain, or suffering. Adolescents, because of their age, may well not have had the experience of weathering difficult times and tend to find it difficult to see current difficulties in perspective. A therapist can offer reassurance that things can and will change. As always, acknowledgment is the necessary building block from which we work. This is critical if the adolescent is to feel understood. Through this exercise, therapists will learn how to build on acknowledgment by offering small changes in language that open up the possibilities for future change.

The purpose of this exercise is to change clients' statements that reflect impossibility and the idea that their situations will not change.

Suggestions for Use

1. This exercise is mainly for therapists but can be given to clients to help them raise their level of awareness regarding the importance of language.
2. As a clinician it's important to tune your ears to words, phrases, or descriptions that suggest impossibility (e.g., "always," "never," etc.).
3. It's important that clients' statements aren't dramatically changed. The idea is to combine pure reflection and acknowledgment with small changes in language that suggest that there are possibilities for change.

Note: This exercise is an adjunct to "Changing Language Through Acknowledgment and Possibility."

EXERCISE

We liken this exercise to the moving walkways in airports. These moving conveyor belts take people to their destinations with little or no effort. We can use language in a similar way to move clients along in the direction of possibilities without them actually having to take steps toward those goals and preferred outcomes. To complete this exercise, use each corresponding method of acknowledging while simultaneously offering possibilities for future change and achieving goals and preferred outcomes.

Part 1

1. *Assume future solutions through future talk.* Assume the possibility of clients and others involved finding solutions; use words such as "yet" and "so far." These words presuppose that even though things feel stuck or unchangeable in the present, they will change sometime in the future. This simple shift in language can help to create a "light at the end of the tunnel."

Examples:

CLIENT: "Things will never go right for me."
THERAPIST: "*So far* things haven't gone right or you."
CLIENT: "I'm always in some kind of trouble."
THERAPIST: "You haven't found a way to stay out of trouble *yet.*"

Client: "Nobody will ever understand me."
Therapist: _____

Client: "I'll never be good at anything."
Therapist: _____

Client: "My life is going downhill."
Therapist: _____

2. *Turning problem statements into goals.* Take client problem statements and change them into a statement about a preferred future or goal. This particular way of changing language serves several purposes. First, it offers a way of acknowledging clients. A second way relates to situations that therapists often find themselves in. That is, in the course of attending and listening to clients' stories, it can become difficult for therapists to discern what is most concerning for clients. Therapists must routinely make decisions regarding which client words, phrases, comments, and remarks should gain more or less attention. By using the method offered here, therapists can acknowledge clients' statements and simultaneously clarify the importance of the statement in clients' eyes.

Examples:

CLIENT: "I'll never have the kind of life that I want."
THERAPIST: "So *you'd like to be able to find a way* to have the kind of life that you want?"
CLIENT: "I'm worthless."
THERAPIST: "So *one of the things that we could do* is to help you to find some self-worth?"

Client: "I'm just not good at school."
Therapist: _____

Client: "I never have fun anymore."
Therapist: _____

Client: "My mom is always on my case."
Therapist: _____

3. *Presupposing changes and progress.* Assume changes and progress toward goals by using words such as "when" and "will." Instead of saying "if" change occurs, we presuppose that it will and build on that expectation of future change.

Examples:

CLIENT: "All I do is get into trouble."

THERAPIST: "So *when* you've put trouble behind you, *you'll* feel as though things are heading in a better direction."

CLIENT: "No one wants to be in a relationship with me."

THERAPIST: "So *when* you get the sense that you have found people who might be interested in having a relationship with you, *we'll* know that we've made some progress."

Client: "I'm always getting angry and saying things I shouldn't say."
Therapist: _____

Client: "Nobody will ever want to hang out with me."
Therapist: _____

Client: "I'll never be a good student."
Therapist: _____

14

Acknowledging Efforts

THERAPIST'S OVERVIEW

Purpose of Exercise

A common complaint of children and adolescents is that their parents don't notice the efforts they make but are quick to find fault. This situation is frequently offered as a reason to avoid putting forth an effort. From the child's point of view, the adults are demanding unilateral change which puts the child in a position of either resisting or "losing" (by doing what the parent wants). You can avoid getting caught in the middle by challenging both sides and adding a bit of humor. This exercise is designed to take the emphasis off the disputed behavior of the adolescent and onto the parents' ability to notice and acknowledge change. The hope is that spreading some of the pressure to perform to the parents can relieve the bind that keeps the child stuck. Frequently, parents are pleased to have a suggestion for useful action.

Suggestions for Use

1. You may want to help the family define the desired behavior in this session.
2. It may be helpful for the family to create a reward for some level of success in this exercise.
3. This exercise works best with the active participation of all parties and is often well-received if presented in a spirit of a challenge or with humor.
4. You may need to make suggestions to the parents on how to acknowledge desired behavior.
5. Remind the child/adolescent that if he or she tries doing something different, parents have no grounds to say that he or she isn't trying.

EXERCISE

People can easily get caught in a situation in which each waits for the other to change. Of course, if change is going to take place, someone is going to have to do something different. This exercise is designed to invite you to reconsider you own behavior and acknowledge efforts made by others.

To complete this exercise, first spell out in detail the behavior that you want. Make sure that it is clear. Break it down into steps if that would be helpful. For the purposes of this exercise, work on only one behavior at a time.

_____

_____

_____

_____

_____

_____

_____

_____

_____

_____

Now list four things that, as a parent, you can say to acknowledge efforts made by your child/adolescent.

1. _____

2. _____

3. _____

4. _____

During the week your child/adolescent will perform the desired behavior at least once per day. (There are no rules against doing it more often.) As a parent, you are to "catch your teen/child in the act" and acknowledge the change. Your child/adolescent will record the things he or she does in the spaces provided below, receiving 1 point for each, and you (the parent) will receive 1 point (to be recorded, as well) if the acknowledgment is made within five minutes of the action. The behavior must be in your full sight for the point to count.

Date	What did you do?	Was it acknowledged?	How?
_____	_____	_____	_____
_____	_____	_____	_____
_____	_____	_____	_____
_____	_____	_____	_____
_____	_____	_____	_____
_____	_____	_____	_____
_____	_____	_____	_____
_____	_____	_____	_____

_____   _____   _____   _____

_____   _____   _____   _____

_____   _____   _____   _____

_____   _____   _____   _____

_____   _____   _____   _____

_____   _____   _____   _____

_____   _____   _____   _____

_____   _____   _____   _____

_____   _____   _____   _____

_____   _____   _____   _____

_____   _____   _____   _____

_____   _____   _____   _____

_____   _____   _____   _____

_____   _____   _____   _____

_____   _____   _____   _____

_____   _____   _____   _____

_____   _____   _____   _____

_____   _____   _____   _____

_____   _____   _____   _____

_____   _____   _____   _____

_____   _____   _____   _____

_____   _____   _____   _____

_____   _____   _____   _____

_____   _____   _____   _____

_____   _____   _____   _____

15

Lenses

THERAPIST'S OVERVIEW

Purpose of the Exercise

When Disneyland was being constructed, Walt Disney used to have the park engineers kneel down on their knees to view an attraction or something he had in mind. Why did he do this? To help them to gain the perspective of children, the most frequent guests at the park. For some people, learning that others see things differently than they do is a revelation. They assume that what they see is the way it is. These assumptions often lead to problems when the other person is acting out of a different viewpoint and "not making sense." Therapy can present parents, children, and adolescents with an opportunity to listen to each other and learn to appreciate all perspectives. In the safety of the therapy session, people will often reveal parts of themselves that they are unwilling to share in a more threatening environment. The purpose of this exercise is to help therapists invite parents, children, and adolescents to begin to share themselves, and see the varying perspectives of others.

Suggestions for Use

1. This exercise might be used as a starting point for family members who have trouble acknowledging one another's point of view.
2. Be prepared to discuss the exercise and to interrupt any attempts at criticism of anyone's point of view.

EXERCISE

Each of us sees our world in different ways. We look through a lens that clarifies and distorts what we see, giving each of us our own personal view of the world. This is wonderful at times and not so great at others. If you are going to learn to understand each other, it might be helpful to get an idea of what lenses you are using. Here is an exercise to help you begin.

To complete this exercise, follow the instructions and record your responses in the spaces provided.

1. Take a family outing (e.g., a walk, dinner out, trip to the mall, etc.).
2. While on your outing, look for your answers to the following questions:

What was the most interesting thing you encountered and why?

_____

_____

_____

_____

What was the most beautiful thing you saw?

_____

_____

_____

_____

What did you find attractive about it?

_____

_____

_____

_____

What was the most repulsive thing you saw?

_____

_____

_____

_____

What about it put you off?

_____

_____

_____

_____

What will you remember about this experience? Why?

_____

_____

_____

_____

At the end of your trip, share your answers with the other family members. Note your own reactions to the responses of the others and share your reactions if you think it would be helpful. For the purposes of this exercise, you may want to try to understand the opinions of others, even if they differ from yours. Also consider these questions as you reflect:

What do your reactions tell you about yourself?

_____

_____

_____

_____

How do you typically react when others have opinions that differ from yours?

_____

_____

_____

_____

What did you learn about yourself from this exercise?

_____

_____

_____

_____

What might you do differently as a result of what you've learned?

_____

_____

_____

_____

16

Sticks and Stones May Break My Bones
but Words Can Hurt Too!
Using Solution-Talk

THERAPIST'S OVERVIEW

Purpose of Exercise

As the fields of psychiatry, psychology, and psychotherapy have evolved, so has the use of jargon. That is, we've become accustomed to using language that emphasizes pathology and deficit with adolescents. Such language can contribute to defensiveness among parents and adolescents as it emphasizes what's wrong as opposed to what's right. It also tends to blame parents and adolescents for problems. We refer to this as "problem-talk."

The purpose of this exercise is to change the basic language that is used when identifying what the concerns are with adolescents and families. To do this we move from problem-talk to "solution-talk." This can do two things:

1. Promote hope by being less stigmatizing and blaming
2. Create new possibilities for dealing with the complaint

This exercise can be used at any point to help parents change their basic language and move from problem-talk to solution-talk. As a mental health professional, you may also choose to do this exercise when you encounter problem-talk in the form of labeling or jargon.

Suggestions for Use

1. This exercise is designed to be given to parents.
2. Give examples to clients of changing problem-talk to solution-talk.
3. Ask clients what new ideas they might have once they begin to use solution-talk.
4. As a clinician, consider what new ideas you might have as a result of using solution-talk.

EXERCISE

The language that we use can either acknowledge and validate or blame and invalidate. In addition, it can close down or open up the possibilities for change. This exercise will help you to challenge the way you describe the behavior that you've observed from your child and/or adolescent. This can help you to see more possibilities for approaching that behavior.

In the left column are examples of problem-talk. The first few responses in the right column are in the form of solution-talk. To complete this exercise, locate the problem-focused term or phrase in the left column and fill in the blank in the corresponding right column by using solution-talk.

Problem-Talk	Solution-Talk
Hyperactive	Very energetic at times
Attention deficit	Short attention span sometimes
Anger problem	Gets upset sometimes
Depressed	Sad
Oppositional	Argues a point often
Rebellious	_____
Disruptive	_____
Negative peer pressure	_____
Isolating	_____
Manipulative	_____

What did you learn by changing the problem-focused terms to solution-talk? _____

_____

_____

_____

_____

Now, plug in your own problem-focused descriptions and change them to solution-talk.

_____	_____
_____	_____
_____	_____
_____	_____
_____	_____
_____	_____

The next time you find yourself using problem-focused descriptions, consider other ways of describing the behavior that you're observing from your child or adolescent. After doing so, see what possibilities become available to you in terms of approaching the behavior you want to see change.

17

Parents' Mission

THERAPIST'S OVERVIEW

Purpose of Exercise

When parents are facing difficulties with their adolescents, things can become unclear at many levels. A lack of clarity can contribute to self-blame or blaming of others, criticism of self and others, and/or unhelpful methods of problem solving. It can also lead parents to forget about their strengths as caregivers and what their intentions are for their adolescents and for themselves.

The purpose of this exercise is to help parents to clarify what they value, find important, and what it is that they feel they do well in regard to parenting. It's also designed to remind parents of the direction they're heading and what they would like to have different in their lives in relation to their adolescent. This exercise can be used at any point in therapy or as a take-home activity as it helps parents to pay attention to what they do well. It can be particularly helpful at the beginning of therapy as a way of getting things off to a good start.

Suggestions for Use

1. Normalize the idea that everyone faces adversity and that in times of trouble we may need to reset our compasses.
2. If parents have trouble identifying strong points, begin to look at areas where things may be going well or holding course. Do not try to convince a parent of his or her strengths. Instead, find moments in that person's life when things went a little better in relation to a problem and then ask: How did you do that? The key is to evoke the strength from the parent's life.
3. To set up the exercise, consider saying to the parents, "The day-to-day issues that arise for you as a parent can make you feel like a ship in a stormy sea. Knowing where you are headed can help you keep your bearings. This exercise will help you develop a clear statement of your intentions. You can refer to this in the future when making decisions in the middle of a foggy night."

EXERCISE

Everyone faces some degree of adversity in life. Yet raising children and adolescents can cause some parents to doubt and unnecessarily blame themselves when trouble arises. This exercise is designed to remind you of what you value, believe to be important, and what you do well as a parent or caregiver.

To complete this exercise, write your responses in the spaces provided.

What are your strongest points as a parent?

1. _____

2. _____

3. _____

What, in your mind, are the most important characteristics of a good parent?

1. _____

2. _____

3. _____

How will you know that you've been a success as a parent? Respond in a way that there will be no doubt.

1. _____

2. _____

3. _____

List five characteristics of the relationship you want to have with your adolescent.

1. _____

2. _____

3. _____

4. _____

5. _____

If you don't have this type of relationship, what makes that difficult?

1. _____

2. _____

3. _____

What are you doing that is counterproductive?

1. _____

2. _____

3. _____

What would you like to be doing instead?

1. _____

2. _____

3. _____

Write a description of what you want to accomplish as a parent, in fifty words or less.

_____

_____

_____

_____

_____

_____

_____

_____

18

Adolescents' Mission

THERAPIST'S OVERVIEW

Purpose of Exercise

It is often assumed that adolescents don't value much, are narcissistic, and don't think about the future. This in an unhelpful perspective and can alienate adolescents from adults. Although adolescents' value systems don't always match their parents' and other adults, nonetheless, they do have values.

The purpose of this exercise is to help adolescents clarify what they value and find important in their lives. It's also designed to help adolescents with the direction they're heading and what they would like to have different in their lives in relation to their futures. This exercise can be used at any point in therapy or as a take-home activity. It can be particularly helpful at the beginning of therapy as a way of getting things off to a good start.

Suggestions for Use

1. Normalize that everyone faces adversity and that in times of trouble we may need to reset our compasses.
2. If adolescents have trouble identifying strong points, begin to look at areas where things may be going well or holding course. Do not try to convince an adolescent of his or her strengths. Instead, find moments in his or her life when things went a little better in relation to a problem and then ask: How did you do that? The key is to evoke the strength from the adolescent's life.
3. To set up the exercise, consider saying to the adolescent, "Even though it may not always be clear to you, there are things that you value and are important to you. By identifying these things you can learn where you want to go down the road, how you can make a difference in the world, and what steps will get you going in the direction you prefer."
4. This exercise is designed to be completed by adolescents.

EXERCISE

Many people go through life making decisions based on how they feel at the moment. Others have very definite plans they follow. In fact, probably most people tend to do a bit of both. This is an exercise to help you clarify some of the things that are important to you. When you are clear on the big picture, you can decide how you will let it guide your day-to-day choices.

In doing this exercise, consider that many adults believe that teenagers don't ever think about or care about the future. Ask yourself whether you want to be stereotyped in that way. The questions that follow can help you to clarify what you value and what's important to you.

To complete this exercise, write your responses in the spaces provided.

What are three things you value about yourself?

1. _____

2. _____

3. _____

List three things others like about you.

1. _____

2. _____

3. _____

What are the three things most valuable about you that go unnoticed or under-recognized by others?

1. _____

2. _____

3. _____

Describe the living situation you want in five years (e.g., work, location, who you'll live with).

_____

_____

_____

Describe the two things that you think might be the primary difficulties in getting the life you want.

1. _____

2. _____

What are three small things you can do to begin moving in the direction you want to go?

1. _____

2. _____

3. _____

Describe three things you plan to do that will change the world.

1. _____

2. _____

3. _____

In fifty words or less, tell what you feel is your purpose on earth.

_____

_____

_____

_____

_____

_____

19

Thinking Out of the Box: Expanding Creativity

THERAPIST'S OVERVIEW

Purpose of Exercise

Walt Disney once said, "The only limitation to animation is your imagination." Therapists and clients can become stuck in how they conceptualize problems and how they go about solving them. Oftentimes, what seems impossible is really a product of one's perspective and personal assumptions. This exercise will assist therapists and clients in thinking "out of the box" to challenge their assumptions and expand their perspectives to think more creatively about how to approach problems.

Suggestions for Use

1. This exercise can be used with therapists, parents, adolescents, or anyone who may need assistance in thinking more creatively.
2. Encourage those trying to complete this exercise to think out of the box or outside the lines.

EXERCISE

This exercise will assist you in challenging your personal assumptions and in getting your creative juices flowing. This can help you to approach the problem you're facing in new ways.

To complete this exercise, you will need a pencil. You may choose to draw directly on this paper or use another blank piece of paper.

Your mission is to connect the nine dots using only four lines and without lifting your pencil off of the paper. Ready, go!

       •   •   •

       •   •   •

       •   •   •

Okay, if you haven't already figured it out, see the next page for the answer.

Answer

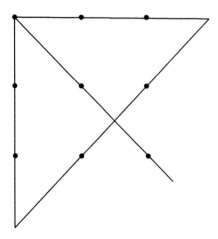

What assumptions did you make that kept you from immediately seeing the solution? _____

_____

_____

_____

_____

What assumptions are you making about the problem you're facing right now? _____

_____

_____

_____

_____

How do your assumptions limit you in searching for a solution to the problem you're facing?

_____

_____

_____

_____

_____

As you develop new ideas and approaches for the problem you're facing, list them in the spaces provided.

1. _____

2. _____

3. _____

4. _____

5. _____

– 20 –

Controlling and Letting Go

THERAPIST'S OVERVIEW

Purpose of the Exercise

Parenting can be seen as a process of letting go. Parents begin with a child who is totally dependent on them and who needs to learn to be self-sufficient. Teaching a child to think and act for himself or herself requires a balance between control and permission. Adjusting to the fact that a child needs to make more decisions and at the same time may make painful mistakes can be difficult for parents who want the best for their child. Controlling too much or too little can have equally negative consequences. This exercise is designed to help parents get clear on what they can and want to control in their child's life.

Suggestions for Use

1. This exercise is designed to be completed by parents.
2. Acknowledge parents' intentions.
3. Discuss the advantages of taking a middle way regarding how much control to exert.
4. Acknowledge the risks of allowing a child to make mistakes.
5. Explore alternative ways for clients to meet the needs of their children.
6. Point out that many important lessons are painful. Blocking natural consequences to protect that child decreases the child's chances of learning.

EXERCISE

Parenting is a balancing act between protecting your child and letting him or her learn in his or her own way. Going too far in either direction causes problems. In addition, as your child ages, your ability to control diminishes. If you try to control areas of your child's life that are simply outside your ability to do so, you will be frustrated. This exercise encourages you to think about what you can control in your child's life and what you really want to control.

To complete this exercise, fill in your answers in the spaces provided. List what you controlled the first week your baby was home. Here are some suggestions to get you started: who the baby associated with; what the baby ate; where the baby was when he or she went to bed; the baby's clothes; etc. Consider these and/or others as you make your list.

_____

_____

_____

_____

_____

What three things most motivated your decisions?

1. _____

2. _____

3. _____

List the five main things in your child's life that you try to control now.

1. _____

2. _____

3. _____

4. _____

5. _____

What motivates you now?

_____

_____

_____

_____

Which of these things do you and your child both wish to control?

_____

_____

_____

_____

What alternatives do you see to controlling your child's behavior other than abandoning your role as a parent?

_____

_____

_____

_____

Bring these responses with you to your next session and discuss them with your counselor.

21

One More One More

THERAPIST'S OVERVIEW

Purpose of the Exercise

Many people who are frustrated may attempt to make changes and, if that fails, give up. Both clients and therapists are lucky when the first intervention is successful. Therapists can increase their chances of success if they can foster a sense of experimentation or perseverance.

The purpose of this exercise is to help parents and adolescents learn to look at experiences as learning opportunities. If you can create an atmosphere in which parents and adolescents cannot fail, you'll find that they are much more willing to take chances, and the likelihood of success will increase. In addition, learning that one can find something of value even in failure is a wonderful lesson that will serve young people throughout their lives.

Suggestions for Use

1. This exercise can be used with parents as well as with adolescents.
2. Maintain your own sense of optimism.
3. Remember that everything the client tells you is important information. Clients' failures tell you as much as their successes.
4. In later sessions, if your client begins to become disheartened, you can return to the responses that were given in this exercise.

EXERCISE

Colonel Sanders called on over 1,000 restaurants before he made the first sale of his recipe for fried chicken. Think about it. He was told "No" over 1,000 times before he got his first sale. The successful person is usually the one who refuses to give up. However, it's often difficult to go back and try again after a failure. Use this exercise to clarify your goals and thinking process to help you bounce back. Do this exercise when you are feeling relatively confident.

To complete this exercise, write your responses to the questions in the spaces provided.

List five things you tell yourself when you are ready to give up.

1. _____

2. _____

3. _____

4. _____

5. _____

Next, prepare a response that challenges each of those statements.

1. _____

2. _____

3. _____

4. _____

5. _____

Ask yourself your reasons for continuing this far. When you are having trouble getting going, ask yourself if your reasons have changed.

Now, write five things that typically help you recharge your energy level.

1. _____

2. _____

3. _____

4. _____

5. _____

Now, remind yourself of people who have inspired you in the past. Write down what they would say to you now.

1. _____

2. _____

3. _____

4. _____

5. _____

Keep this in a place where you can find it when you need it. You'll know how to use it when the time comes.

22

Teach Your Children

THERAPIST'S OVERVIEW

Purpose of the Exercise

Parents often get discouraged when their children and/or adolescents do not behave as they wish. Parents frequently accuse them of "trying to get attention" or "having an attitude." Usually, this attitude on the part of the parents does not increase the likelihood of finding a solution and often works in the opposite direction.

The purpose of this exercise is to encourage parents to consider the possibility that their child's or adolescent's motivation may not be negative, but is simply different from their own. It encourages parents to consider their child's or adolescent's behavior as a form of communication that informs them about what the child still needs to learn.

Suggestions for Use

1. This exercise is intended to be used with parents.
2. Suggest to the parents that one of their major roles is to be teachers for their children and adolescents. Their behavior lets them know how to formulate their teaching plan.
3. Ask parents about exceptions to the times when their children or adolescents have acted out of negative motivation. Explore with them how they respond when they believe that their children or adolescents are acting with positive intentions.
4. Challenge clients to consider the effect on their children or adolescents when they believe their children have negative intentions.

EXERCISE

Your understanding of your child's or adolescent's behavior will probably affect how you respond. If you really think that he or she was "trying to help" you will act differently than if he or she was "trying to get attention." The more you can see your child's or adolescent's good intentions, the better you will be able to respond in a helpful way.

To complete this exercise, each day write down one thing your child or adolescent did that you did not approve of and follow it with your explanation of why he or she acted this way.

For each day:

Child/adolescent's behavior:

_____

_____

My explanation of the behavior:

_____

_____

How does your explanation affect your own response?

_____

_____

How would it change your response if you saw this behavior as evidence of a need for more training rather than something negative on the child's or adolescent's part? That is, what would you do differently if you saw the negative behavior differently? Be as specific as possible.

_____

_____

_____

_____

_____

_____

_____

_____

_____

Whenever you see your child's or adolescent's behavior as purely negative consider doing this exercise to help you generate new ways of looking at and dealing with the behavior.

23

Who Are You? Exploring the Qualities Within

THERAPIST'S OVERVIEW

Purpose of Exercise

In many cases, people continue to move from day to day despite the odds they face. However, they don't always notice what those qualities and actions are that enable them to do so. By orienting parents, children, and adolescents toward these aspects of themselves, it's possible to help them change views they have of themselves and their situations, and to use those resources to deal with future adversity.

The purpose of this exercise is twofold. First, it can help parents, children, and adolescents to identify those qualities that allow them to manage adversity. Second, it helps clients to identify actions that those qualities allow them to undertake. Oftentimes, these qualities and associated actions are helpful in resolving the concerns that clients are facing in the present.

Suggestions for Use

1. This exercise can be used with parents, children, and adolescents.
2. Resilient qualities can be present within individuals and/or relationships.
3. We are not trying to convince clients of anything. We are not saying, "Don't you see all the wonderful qualities that you have?" That's invalidating to people who are suffering and in pain. Instead, clients are convincing us by answering our questions. They are doing their own self-inventories and tapping into their personal resources. This allows for clients to change views and attribute change or "control" to their personal qualities, internal abilities and resources, and actions.

EXERCISE

This exercise will assist you in two ways. First, it will help you identify qualities you possess or those that exist in your relationships with others that allow you to manage the adversity you face in your life. These qualities can be of assistance to you in resolving your concerns or problems with your children and/or adolescents. Second, it will help you identify how those qualities allow you to stand up to adversity.

To complete this exercise, take a moment to consider the following questions. Then, write your responses in the spaces provided.

What qualities do you possess that allow you to move through life? To be a child yourself? A brother or sister? A mother or father? A parent? A grandparent? An uncle or aunt? A friend? A co-worker or colleague? A boss? Other role?

_____

_____

_____

_____

_____

What would others say are the qualities that you have that keep you going?

_____

_____

_____

_____

_____

What do those qualities say about the kind of person you are?

_____

_____

_____

_____

_____

How do those qualities help you in times of trouble?

_____

_____

_____

_____

_____

What have the qualities allowed you to do that you might not have otherwise done?

_____

_____

_____

_____

_____

When facing difficulties, consider how the qualities that you possess allow you to take action to get the upper hand with those difficulties.

24

Catch Your Child/Adolescent Doing Well

THERAPIST'S OVERVIEW

Purpose of Exercise

In the midst of problems with children and adolescents, it's easy to notice only when problems are happening. However, there are almost always times when children and adolescents are behaving more the way we'd like. Oftentimes, these positive moments go unnoticed, as their appearances are more infrequent than the problematic ones. Yet if we only pay attention to what's not working, we miss opportunities to identify what is working and, perhaps, solutions to the problems being faced.

The purpose of this exercise is to help parents to identify times when their children or adolescents are being "good" or acting more the way they'd like. This can show parents that most behaviors do not happen "24-7" and, that at times, their kids act in ways that meet with their approval.

Suggestions for Use

1. This exercise is intended for use with parents.
2. It's important that clinicians acknowledge the difficulties that clients are experiencing before helping to identify when their kids are behaving or doing well. If this does not occur, clients will feel that clinicians do not understand the severity of their problems or are giving short shrift to them.
3. Before moving on to specific problem areas, it may be helpful to begin broadly by suggesting that parents catch their kids doing well at just about anything. This can help them to shift their views to focusing on what's right as opposed to what's wrong.

EXERCISE

It's very easy to identify when things aren't going well and when problems are present. In fact, many of us could be certified "problem identifiers." What we aren't always so polished in is noticing when things are going well and our children and adolescents are doing well. This exercise will help you to become more adept at identifying when your kids are acting more the way you'd like.

To complete this exercise, write your response to each inquiry in the spaces provided.

Over the next week, notice when your son or daughter is engaging in behaviors that meet with your approval. In other words, as much as possible, try and catch your son or daughter "being good." You may want to keep track of the behaviors you've observed and write them down in the spaces provided.

1. _____

2. _____

3. _____

4. _____

5. _____

6. _____

7. _____

8. _____

9. _____

10. _____

For each of the behaviors you listed, devise a response that will let your son or daughter know that you like what they are doing. Be specific about the words you use and remember that communication can take many forms.

1. _____

2. _____

3. _____

4. _____

5. _____

6. _____

7. _____

8. _____

9. _____

10. _____

As you reflect back on the behaviors and actions that you observed your son or daughter doing well, what do those behaviors tell you about him or her?

_____

_____

_____

_____

_____

Now be more specific. Over the next week, notice when your son or daughter is demonstrating the behavior that you prefer, as opposed to the undesirable or problem behavior that you want to see change. In doing this, what did you notice?

_____

_____

_____

_____

_____

After completing this exercise, review your answers. What did you notice happening with your child or adolescent when he or she was acting more the way you'd like? What does that tell you about your son or daughter? What did you learn? Consider how your answers might help you in finding solutions to the problem you've been facing.

_____

_____

_____

_____

_____

25

Everyday Is an Exception

THERAPIST'S OVERVIEW

Purpose of Exercise

This exercise involves helping parents to notice times when the problem they're facing with their son or daughter happens less frequently, is less intense or dominating, or absent altogether. These times represent exceptions to the problem. By identifying exceptions, parents can learn that problems do not happen "all the time." There are times when problems are more manageable and when parents, children, and adolescents have influence over them.

The purpose of this exercise is to help parents notice times when things go differently in regard to the problem. This can help them to gain a different perspective on the problems they're facing and perhaps approach solving them in new ways.

Suggestions for Use

1. This exercise is intended for use with parents.
2. It's often helpful to explain to clients that problems typically ebb and flow. That is, there are times when they are more or less dominating. Let clients know that you would like to explore the times when they have had some influence over the problem(s) they are facing.
3. Before suggesting this exercise, it's important that you acknowledge and validate clients' feelings. That is, make sure that they know that you understand the pain and suffering they have been experiencing. Then suggest noticing small changes as opposed to all or nothing experiences with the problem. We don't want to imply, "When doesn't the problem happen?" Many will respond, "It always happens!" and may experience some level of invalidation. For example, a therapist might say, "You've been through a lot over the past few months. It sounds like it's been very hard on you. So that we can really understand when the problem is *just a little less* dominating in your life, would you be open to trying an experiment for the next week?" This way we are acknowledging the parents' experiences with the problem and suggesting an exercise to determine variances with it. This will more likely be palatable to the parents.
4. This is a good exercise to use at any point in therapy when a parent seems to be struggling to identify times when things went a little different in regard to the problem.

EXERCISE

Even though problems can seem to happen "all the time" and "never" let up, if we pay close attention, each day we can find that there are times when things go just a little better. There will be times that the problem was less intrusive or absent altogether.

This exercise will help you to identify times when things went a little better regarding problems you're facing with your adolescent or teenager. To complete this exercise, over the next week, notice times when the problem happened less frequently, was a little less intense, or was absent altogether. Then, in the spaces provided for each day, write what happened *instead* of the problem showing up in its usual form. Be specific in describing what behaviors you observed.

In addition, on a scale of 1 to 10, with 1 representing the worst the problem could be and 10 representing no problem at all, rate each situation.

Day 1   What Happened?   **Rating**

        1. _____   _____

        2. _____   _____

        3. _____   _____

Day 2   What Happened?   **Rating**

        1. _____   _____

        2. _____   _____

        3. _____   _____

Day 3   What Happened?   **Rating**

        1. _____   _____

        2. _____   _____

        3. _____   _____

Day 4   What Happened?   **Rating**

        1. _____   _____

        2. _____   _____

        3. _____   _____

Day 5   What Happened?   **Rating**

        1. _____   _____

        2. _____   _____

        3. _____   _____

Day 6   **What Happened?**   **Rating**

     1. _____ _____

     2. _____ _____

     3. _____ _____

Day 7   **What Happened?**   **Rating**

     1. _____ _____

     2. _____ _____

     3. _____ _____

Take a moment to look over the results from the past week. What did you notice about your son or daughter's behavior? What did you learn? How can that be helpful to you in approaching the problem?

_____

_____

_____

_____

_____

_____

_____

_____

_____

If you are in counseling, bring this to your next appointment.

26

Searching for "Counter" Evidence

THERAPIST'S OVERVIEW

Purpose of Exercise

This exercise involves getting clients or others who know them to tell you something that doesn't fit with their problematic stories. This can include times when the problem is less intrusive or dominant in the person's life or completely absent. To find counterevidence, the therapist explores with the client and others aspects of the person's life, events, or situations to identify such evidence.

The purpose of this exercise is to help clients to identify times when things have gone differently in regard to their problem descriptions. This can help them to notice that there are times that they have had influence over their problems. Once counterevidence has been identified, it can be explored with clients how they can utilize that influence over their problems in the present.

Suggestions for Use

1. It's often helpful to explain to clients that problems typically have an ebb and flow to them. That is, there are times when they are more or less dominating. Let clients know that you would like to explore the times when they have had some influence over the problem(s) they are facing.
2. First, try searching for counterevidence in the present. If it is difficult to find any exceptions in recent times, gradually move backward in time. To do this you might ask, "How far back would you have to go to find a time when the problem wasn't so dominant in your life?" Once counterevidence has been identified, explore with the client what it would take to bring forth the exceptions from the past in order to have some influence over the problem in the present.

EXERCISE

When people are in pain, they tend to focus their attention on the pain they are feeling. The psychiatrist, Milton Erickson, used to remind people in pain that there were parts of their bodies that weren't feeling any pain at that moment. As soon as they would reorient their attention to those parts of their bodies, they would often find that they would feel less pain. Why? Because when we have problems, we fixate our attention on them. For example, when we're depressed, we often focus our attention on all the horrible things we've done or felt, or on our failures in the past. In searching for counterevidence, we want to help clients shift their attention to explore times in their lives when their problems have been less dominating.

What was different before the problem began to have such an influence in your life?

_____

_____

_____

_____

Describe a time in the recent past (a few days, weeks ago) when the problem wasn't as dominating or disruptive in your life. What specifically happened?

_____

_____

_____

_____

If you had a difficult time with Question #2, how far back would you have to go to find a time when things went just a little better in regard to the problem you're facing? What happened? What did you do differently?

_____

_____

_____

_____

What did you learn from your answers to the previous questions that might be helpful to you in the present?

_____

_____

_____

_____

What might you do differently in facing your problem as a result of what you've learned?

_____

_____

_____

_____

27

One of These Things Is Not Like the Other

THERAPIST'S OVERVIEW

Purpose of Exercise

Adolescents are notorious for saying one thing and doing another. Still, if we challenge them by saying, "You say this and do that!" it's unlikely that we will get anywhere. The purpose of this exercise is to subtly and respectfully challenge adolescents' views and subsequent actions so that they come to their own conclusions that something has to change. By allowing adolescents to save face and create their own new perspectives, we increase the chances of them changing for the better.

Suggestions for Use

1. This exercise can be most useful with older children and adolescents and is to be completed by the therapist.
2. Be careful to not blame or lecture adolescents. They typically tune out such conversations.
3. It can be useful to play "dumb" during this exercise. To do this simply say, " I don't get it and I usually pick up on these things quickly. You say that this is what you want, yet what you've been doing doesn't seem to be getting you there. Help me to understand what I'm missing."
4. Don't worry about adolescents responding with "I don't know." Merely by asking questions of them they will at least think about them.

EXERCISE

This exercise will assist in subtly and respectfully challenging adolescents to reconsider the way they are going about achieving their goals or solving a problem. If we directly say, "You say one thing and do another" it is unlikely that they will change their views or actions as they will feel threatened or blamed. This exercise will help adolescents to save face and make changes on their own. At the same time, they can experience the inner ability to change course at any time.

To complete this exercise, take a moment to ask adolescents one or more of the following inquiries. Then, write their responses in the spaces provided. You may choose to jump to a specific question that is more consistent with where you are at the moment.

Tell me about how you've approached the problem you are facing so far.

_____

_____

_____

_____

I'm curious, how has taking that approach helped you?

_____

_____

_____

_____

I usually understand things pretty well, but I must be missing something here. You've told me that you want to _____ in the future. But I need you to help me to understand how doing _____ is going to get you to where you want to be. What am I not getting right here?

_____

_____

_____

_____

You seem to have a plan, but others may not understand it as clearly as you do. How would you explain your plan for _____ in a way that they would get it?

_____

_____

_____

_____

If you find that what you're doing isn't working as well as you had planned, what do you think you'll do?

_____

_____

_____

_____

If you changed your plan of dealing with _____, how would you get yourself to follow through with it?

_____

_____

_____

_____

What would be your first step in putting your new plan in to motion?

_____

_____

_____

_____

28

How Else Might You See It?
Exploring Alternative Perspectives

THERAPIST'S OVERVIEW

Purpose of Exercise

At times, parents' interpretations, explanations, and evaluations of themselves, others, events, or situations close down the possibilities for change. Parents act in ways that are consistent with rigid views. Young people may simply have limited experiences that limit the way they see things. In these cases, in an effort to dissolve the problematic story, it can be helpful to offer a different point of view. It is essential that therapists do not state different points of views as facts or truths. In other words, we want to give parents the space to accept or reject all or part of therapists' interpretations.

The purpose of this exercise is to subtly challenge the problematic perspectives that are held by parents, by offering new, alternative views that offer possibilities for change. If parents change their frames of reference, their actions are more likely to be in accordance with those views.

Suggestions for Use

1. This exercise is intended for use with parents or other caregivers.
2. This exercise can be given to parents, or can be used by mental health professionals to help generate new views.
3. Alternative stories that are offered to parents should adhere to the same facts yet offer new perspectives which allow parents to view their situations differently. It is hoped that new views of parents' situations will lead to new actions and positive change.
4. If new frames don't fit the client it is OK. The idea is to generate new views of situations that will allow parents to approach their concerns differently.

EXERCISE

Often, the explanations we have for the problems we're facing with our children and adolescents are part of the problem. In fact, our explanations may lead us in unhelpful directions without our knowing it. On the other hand, new explanations for the same problems can help us to approach them differently. This exercise will help you to challenge your current explanations and create some new ones. You can then determine how those new explanations might help you to change what you do to solve the problems you're facing.

What explanation do you have for the problem(s) that you are currently experiencing with your child or adolescent?

_____

_____

_____

_____

How does your explanation influence the way that you approach solving your problem(s)?

_____

_____

_____

_____

What other possible explanations might you consider regarding the same problem? List five alternative explanations for the problem you're facing. Be creative.

1. _____

2. _____

3. _____

4. _____

5. _____

Go through your list of alternative explanations and rule out those that a neutral person would judge to be less than 50 percent likely.

For each alternative explanation, list three ways that your behavior would change if you were to adopt that explanation.

1. _____

    a. _____

    b. _____

    c. _____

2. _____

    a. _____

    b. _____

    c. _____

3. _____

    a. _____

    b. _____

    c. _____

4. _____

    a. _____

    b. _____

    c. _____

5. _____

    a. _____

    b. _____

    c. _____

For each behavior change, write down what would be the effect of changing your behavior in that way right now.

1. _____

    a. _____

    b. _____

    c. _____

2. _____

    a. _____

    b. _____

    c. _____

3. _____

    a. _____

    b. _____

    c. _____

4. _____

    a. _____

    b. _____

    c. _____

5. _____

    a. _____

    b. _____

    c. _____

As a way of experimenting with and testing out alternative explanations, for the next few days or week, select one new explanation and try acting "as if" that explanation were true regarding your problem. For example, if you believed that your son was manipulating you to get his way and that explanation wasn't helpful, you might consider that he was wanting more attention from you. By trying out the latter explanation or theory you might get a different result. If one explanation doesn't lead to the outcome you desire, try another. Be sure to pay close attention to those explanations that lead to the results for which you are looking.

– 29 –

At the Movies

THERAPIST'S OVERVIEW

Purpose of Exercise

There are many mediums that can help parents, children, and adolescents to change their perspectives from those that are closed to perspectives that afford choice and are more open. One specific medium is movies. By having parents, children, adolescents, and entire families watch movies (or TV shows), they can often develop new ways of viewing their current problems. They can also access their own previous solutions that may have been long forgotten.

The purpose of this exercise is to help parents, children, and adolescents view their problems or situations differently through the use of motion pictures. By changing their views, some will take new actions in facing their problems.

Suggestions for Use

1. This exercise can be used individually with parents, children, or adolescents or with entire families.
2. Be sure that if you are suggesting a movie for a child or adolescent that you have parental approval. In addition, be sure to note film ratings.
3. Be sure to view the film, video, or TV show first before recommending it.
4. It's a good idea to remain fairly neutral in the directions that you give to individuals and families. Allow them to create their own meanings rather than suggesting that they learn something in particular.
5. You may want to consult with other clinicians about their choices of movies and in what situations they would or would not use them.
6. Create your own list of movies and note which ones seem to get what kinds of results.

EXERCISE

Most people enjoy the movies. Why? There are many reasons. One is that they allow us to escape from our personal realities for a while. Another is that they entertain us. Have you ever been inspired or touched by a movie? If so, this exercise may help you to change your perspective on the problem you've been facing.

This exercise is meant to help you to create some new ideas, challenge old ones, remember previous solutions to problems, and to explore new possibilities for current problems. You can complete this exercise by yourself, with one of your children or adolescents, or as an entire family. You may also suggest that your son or daughter watch a specific movie on his or her own.

To complete this exercise, follow the directions. Then provide answers to the questions in the spaces provided.

Choose a movie by yourself or with your therapist. The movie should be one that you haven't seen before or haven't seen in a very long time. It is not always necessary, but you might want to choose a movie that in some way relates to the problem you're facing. Here is a brief list of examples:

For Children

The Tigger Movie—adoption, blended families
Simon Birch—dealing with disabilities, learning to cope, making friends, finding hope (for adolescents as well)

For Adolescents

Hoop Dreams—facing adversity, growing up
Angus—trying to fit in, growing up, loss
The Mighty—dealing with disabilities, facing adversity, making friends (for children as well)
The War—facing poverty, making friends, dealing with adversity, loss
Good Will Hunting—physical and emotional abuse, finding a way in life, creating hope

For Parents

Losing Isaiah—adoption, custody
Stand and Deliver—facing poverty, prejudice, resiliency, standing up for what you believe, being committed to others, creating hope
Lorenzo's Oil—chronic illness, resiliency, creative problem solving, creating hope
Dangerous Minds—facing poverty, prejudice, multicultural awareness, creating hope
Ordinary People—grief, loss, divorce
Parenthood—parent-child relationships
Fly Away Home—parent-child relationships
Searching for Bobby Fischer—parent-child relationships (for children as well)

Watch the movie (or TV show). Then, within a few hours of watching the movie, answer the following questions.

What aspect of the movie you watched affected you the most?

_____

_____

_____

_____

_____

How did the movie touch you personally?

_____

_____

_____

_____

_____

What did you learn or were reminded of by the movie?

_____

_____

_____

_____

_____

How might you put those new insights to work with the problem you're facing?

_____

_____

_____

_____

_____

Do you have any other new ideas since watching the movie? If so, what are they?

_____

_____

_____

_____

_____

Consider talking about what you've learned with other family members and/or your therapist.

30

How Come Things Aren't Worse?

Purpose of Exercise

In the midst of intense difficulty or when clients don't feel that they are making progress in regard to their problems, frustration, anxiety, and anger can intensify. Even though parents, children, and adolescents may not feel that they are making progress in the direction of their goals and preferred outcomes, they have inner and relational qualities that keep them from "bottoming out."

The purpose of this exercise is to help clients to identify those qualities and/or actions that allow them to keep going despite the fact that they see things as getting worse.

Suggestions for Use

1. This exercise can be used with parents, children, and adolescents.
2. A search for "coping" qualities and actions can be present within individuals and/or relationships.
3. We want to acknowledge and validate clients' concerns and in effect, join their pessimism. We are saying, "It seems that you have been having a very hard time. And I wonder, what's kept things from completely bottoming out?"

EXERCISE

This exercise will assist you in identifying those qualities and actions that allow you and your family to keep things from hitting rock bottom. Even though it may seem to you that progress is not being made toward your goals or that things are getting worse, there are things that keep you and/or your family afloat. These things may be of assistance to you in turning your relationship around, and with the problems you've been facing.

To complete this exercise, take a moment to consider the following questions. Then, write your responses in the spaces provided.

How come things aren't worse with your situation?

_____

_____

_____

_____

_____

What have you done to keep things from getting worse?

_____

_____

_____

_____

_____

What specific steps have you taken to prevent things from heading downhill any further? Please list these steps.

_____

_____

_____

_____

_____

How has that made a difference for you/with your situation?

_____

_____

_____

_____

_____

Based on your other responses, what is the smallest thing that you could do that might make a difference with your situation?

_____

_____

_____

_____

_____

What would it take to get that to happen a little bit now?

_____

_____

_____

_____

When situations do not seem to be improving or are getting worse, refer back to this sheet.

31

Standing Up to Problems

THERAPIST'S OVERVIEW

Purpose of Exercise

In some cases, problematic views and stories seem to take on a life of their own. The child or adolescent *becomes the problem*. He or she identifies himself or herself as the problem, or others label him or her as "problem." This implies that the child or adolescent is characterologically flawed or "bad." One way to change these stories and the viewing of problems is through the use of *externalizing*. This method is especially useful when children or adolescents already have diagnoses and labels, particularly those that haven't been empowering, validating, or facilitative of the change process.

The purpose of this exercise is to help people to view themselves as separate from problems, to challenge actions, interactions, and ways of thinking that are blaming or unhelpful. This enables them to experience their association with problems differently, allowing for the emergence of a new view and story.

Suggestions for Use

1. This exercise can be used with anyone, but it can be particularly useful with children and adolescents.
2. In naming the problem, younger children will do better with names such as "Mr. Temper Tantrum" or "Ms. Ing Homework." However, with older children and adolescents, it's typically better to simply name the problem as it is, "Fighting," "Incomplete Homework," and so on.
3. It's important to note that the language used here is not deterministic: The problem never *causes or makes* the person or the family do anything, it only *influences, invites, tells, tries to convince, uses tricks, tries to recruit, etc.*
4. If people have a hard time with the language or with the concept, move on to another exercise. Although this is a creative exercise, not everything works with everyone.

EXERCISE

When problems are present with children and adolescents, it can seem as if the children or adolescents have become problems. In actuality, the child or adolescent is never the problem. The problem is the problem. This exercise is designed to help you to identify the problem that has intruded upon your child or adolescent and its effects on your family. This can allow you to learn more about the tactics of the problem and times when things have gone differently. This exercise will require some creativity on your part. Are you ready?

To complete this exercise, take a moment to consider the following questions. Then, write your responses in the spaces provided.

Name the problem. Either as an individual or as a family, give the problem a name that accurately depicts it.

Examples

Temper Tantrums—Mr./Ms. Tantrum
Truancy—Mr. I. B. Truant
Fighting—Fighting

Name of the problem:

_____

Personify the problem and attribute bad intentions and tactics to it. Consider how the problem has made its way into your life.

Questions to Consider

- How long has _____ been trying to convince you to lead a life you don't agree with?
- When did _____ first come over to visit without permission?
- When did you first notice _____ lingering around and making noise?

_____

_____

_____

_____

Investigate how the problem has been disrupting, dominating, or discouraging you and/or your family. How have you felt dominated or forced by the problem to do or experience things you didn't like? Be sure that each person who is involved has the opportunity to speak about the effects of the problem on him or her.

Questions to Consider

- How has _____ come between you and your family/friends, etc?
- When has _____ recruited you into something that you later got in trouble for?
- What intentions do you think _____ has for you?

_____

_____

_____

_____

Discover moments when you and your family haven't been dominated or discouraged by the problem or have not been disrupted by the problem. Describe moments of choice or success that have occurred in regard to the problem. These moments represent times when you and/or others haven't been dominated or cornered by the problem or experienced things you didn't like.

Questions to Consider:

- When have you been able to stand up to _____?
- When has _____ whispered in your ear but you didn't listen?
- Tell me about times when _____ couldn't convince you to _____?

_____

_____

_____

_____

_____

Find evidence from the past to support a new view of you as competent enough to have stood up to, defeated, or escaped from the dominance or oppression of the problem. Search for stories and evidence from the past to show that you were actually competent, strong, and spirited, but didn't always realize it.

Questions to Consider

- What qualities do you think you possess that help you to stand up to _____ plans for you?
- Who are you that you were able to reject _____ taunting?
- How do you explain that you are the kind of person who would lodge a protest against _____?
- What do you think _____ would say if he/she could hear you talk about standing up to _____?
- Who is someone who has known all along that you had the wherewithal to take your life back from the grasp of _____?

_____

_____

_____

_____

_____

Speculate about what kind of future is to be expected from you. Speculate on what future developments will result now that you have evidence that you can influence the problem, and what changes will result as you keep resisting the problem.

Questions to Consider

- As_____ continues to stand up to _____, how do you think that will affect his or her relationships with family members?
- As you continue to keep the upper hand with _____, what do you think will be different about_____, compared to what _____ had planned for you?
- How do you think your strategy with _____ will help you in the future?

Find or create a way of sharing your new identity and new story with others. Using letters, asking for advice from other people suffering from the same or similar problems, arranging for meetings with family members and friends, or through other means, consider ways that others can experience the new story that has evolved.

Questions to Consider

- Who else needs to know about the stance you've taken against _____?
- Who needs to know that you've made a commitment to keep _____ from hanging out without parental permission?
- Who could benefit from knowing about your enlistment in the _____ club?

_____

_____

_____

_____

_____

32

Changing Criticism to Requests or Demands

THERAPIST'S OVERVIEW

Purpose of the Exercise

Most of us don't handle criticism well, no matter how well-intentioned it may be. It tends to put the critic in a dominant position and most of us don't like being one-down. In addition, although criticism clarifies what we don't want, it often doesn't state what we are asking for. The criticized person feels put down or disrespected and may not know how to rectify things. Parents may feel that the solution is or should be obvious to their children and adolescents. If parenting is seen as primarily a job of teaching, it becomes clear that something more than pointing out shortcomings is often needed. This exercise encourages and reminds parents to go beyond criticism and encourage the child toward more desirable behavior.

Suggestions for Use

1. This exercise is for parents.
2. Be prepared to ask the parent to state the desired behavior whenever a complaint is made.
3. That is, what do they want to see happening instead of the complaint or problem. Action-talk can be useful here.
4. Challenge attributions of negative intention.
5. Explore the behaviors that the parent sees as desirable and develop options.

EXERCISE

Children and adolescents don't typically respond well to criticism. Even positive criticism is likely to arouse defensiveness in them. This exercise will help you reduce the amount of criticism you use with your child, adolescent, or others and still get the message across that you desire. To do this, you will need to change your criticism to a request or demand for action.

To complete this exercise, first list five instances when you frequently criticize your child or adolescent or he or she feels criticized.

1. _____

2. _____

3. _____

4. _____

5. _____

Next, for each instance, list exactly what you typically say and do.

1. _____

2. _____

3. _____

4. _____

5. _____

Now, change your words or actions to a request or demand (depending on the situation) that makes no judgment on the child's intentions or character. If you are making a demand, be prepared to issue a consequence if it is not met.

Examples:

"I would like you to clean your room before going to your friend's house."
"It's ok if you're angry but it's not ok to yell at me. Please lower your voice and I will hear what you have to say."

1. _____

2. _____

3. _____

4. _____

5. _____

The next time these issues arise, experiment with making a request instead of criticism. Avoid the temptation to lecture. If you impose consequences, let the consequences speak for you.

You may use the rest of this page to record your experiences so that you don't forget them when you see your therapist.

– 33 –

The Big Picture

THERAPIST'S OVERVIEW

Purpose of Exercise

Sometimes it's helpful to think of behavior as an attempt to meet a need. If there is no push or pull to change, it doesn't happen. Therapy often takes the form of helping clients choose the need with the highest priority and decide how to meet it. Situational needs and desires frequently conflict with long-range goals. We have found that many people get caught up with daily concerns and do not think about "the big picture" for years at a time. Adolescents often have not taken the time to create a big picture. Often, it is helpful to define one's purpose as a way of putting everyday matters into perspective.

Suggestions for Use

1. This exercise has two parts. One is for parents and the other is for adolescents. They can be done together or separately.
2. Keep in mind that there may be value in simply raising these questions. Clients may not have answers now but may continue to work on them long after therapy is complete.
3. Remind clients, particularly adolescents, that this can be a work in progress and is likely to undergo some major changes over time.
4. In reviewing clients' responses to these exercises, you may want to challenge them to create a definitive mission statement for their lives.
5. Link the clients' responses to everyday behaviors that move them toward their goals.
6. Invite clients to find ways to remind themselves of this exercise when they most need it.

EXERCISE

Part 1—For Parents

Most parents begin raising children with high hopes and, of course, little experience. Big dreams and expectations can easily get forgotten in the trivial and great demands of everyday life. In other cases, and for a variety of reasons, plans need to be altered, abandoned, or replaced. If you don't take the time to clarify an overall plan for yourself and with a partner, you risk losing a sense of direction. This exercises invites you to think about some issues that may help you define your sense of direction.

To complete this exercise, write your responses in the spaces provided.

112

What are five qualities of a good parent?

1. _____

2. _____

3. _____

4. _____

5. _____

Name three ways that children/adolescents learn.

1. _____

2. _____

3. _____

List in order the five methods you have learned to teach your child/adolescent.

1. _____

2. _____

3. _____

4. _____

5. _____

How do you want your children to describe you to their grandchildren?

_____

_____

_____

_____

_____

List five ways that will let you know that you were a successful parent when your adolescent leaves home.

1. _____

2. _____

3. _____

4. _____

5. _____

Part 2—For Adolescents

This exercise contains some questions that may be challenging for you. They ask you to begin thinking about issues that each individual either answers or actively avoids answering throughout life. These questions invite you to define for yourself what is valuable so that you can make decisions that range in importance from deciding what to eat for lunch to whether or not you should enter the army.

If you knew that the world was to end tomorrow, what are three things that you would do today?

1. _____

2. _____

3. _____

What was the most meaningful thing you have done in the past month?

_____

_____

_____

_____

_____

List three people (besides yourself) who you think are doing something worthwhile with their lives. What are they doing and why is that important?

1. _____

2. _____

3. _____

List five things you would like to be remembered for.

1. _____

2. _____

3. _____

4. _____

5. _____

What are five things you do now to make that come true?

1. _____

2. _____

3. _____

4. _____

5. _____

What are things you might do in the future to help make that come true?

_____

_____

_____

_____

_____

Why Am I Here . . . and Not on Mars?

THERAPIST'S OVERVIEW

Purpose of Exercise

Existentialist Viktor Frankl talked about the importance of having meaning in our lives. Because parents can become so engulfed in the everyday task of raising children they often don't have or take the time to think about what moves them and what they're on the planet for. In turn, when parents have some meaning in their lives, it can reenergize them, reset their compasses, and help them to see new possibilities for the future.

The purpose of this exercise is to help parents to create or rehabilitate a sense of meaning in their lives. This can influence how they approach their lives in the present.

Suggestions for Use

1. This exercise can be helpful with parents who seem to be in need of a second wind. A sense of meaning can give them more energy and a new sense of direction and commitment.
2. If parents struggle with this exercise, don't worry. Suggest that the questions need some time to percolate within them.

EXERCISE

Have you ever wondered why you are on this planet? Or, what is your mission in life? When we have meaning in our lives things can change dramatically. We can find ourselves with more energy, a new sense of direction, and a renewed commitment to solving the problems that we're facing in our lives and with our children and adolescents. This exercise will challenge you to find out what is important to you and how you derive meaning in life. It may also help you to gain some new ideas that can help you with the problems you're facing.

To complete this exercise, take a moment to consider the following questions. Then, write your responses in the spaces provided.

What do you think you're on this planet for?

_____

_____

What dreams did you or do you have for yourself in upcoming days/weeks/months/years/life?

_____

_____

What do you still need to accomplish during your adult years? As a parent/spouse/sibling, etc.?

_____

_____

In what area do you think you could make a contribution?

_____

_____

What would you try to do with your life if you knew that you could not fail?

_____

_____

What do you need to do to accomplish what you'd like and to make your dreams come true? How can you set that in motion and do that a little bit now?

_____

_____

_____

_____

List the ten most important people in your life and how they would remember you if you were to leave the planet today.

1. _____

2. _____

3. _____

4. _____

5. _____

6. _____

7. _____

8. _____

9. _____

10. _____

How would you like to be remembered by these people?

_____

_____

_____

_____

_____

List five ways that the world is a better place because you existed.

1. _____

2. _____

3. _____

4. _____

5. _____

Between now and your next session, make a list of the things that you did that made you feel worthwhile.

1. _____

2. _____

3. _____

4. _____

5. _____

Refer back to this exercise in the future when you are doubting yourself or your place in the world and where you're going. Also consider talking with your therapist about this exercise and/or how you gain meaning from life.

35

What About the Future?

THERAPIST'S EXERCISE

Purpose of Exercise

Adolescents are often tabbed as having no sense of the future. For some adolescents, the future may be tomorrow. For others, there is a concern about what will happen to them "down the road." A solution-oriented approach holds that clients' visions of the future can have a direct impact on what happens to them in the present.

The purpose of this exercise is to help adolescents who seem to be going "nowhere fast" to create or rehabilitate a sense of the future. By doing so, it is our contention that visions of the future can influence how adolescents approach their lives in the present.

Suggestions for Use

1. This exercise is primarily for adolescents but can also be modified for use with other clientele.
2. Even if adolescents respond with "I don't know" don't be phased. Simply asking them questions will get them thinking.

EXERCISE

A long-held belief is that whatever has happened to you in the past will directly affect what happens to you in the future. This exercise challenges that myth by helping you to see how your vision of the future can affect what you do in the present. For example, if you knew that you were going to be given $10,000,000 tomorrow, would you go to school? Do your homework? If you knew that someone you cared about was going to get hurt and you could save them, would you? By knowing the future, your actions in the present can be determined. This exercise will help you to identify what you want for yourself in the future and how you can begin to move in the direction of your goals and preferred outcomes.

To complete this exercise, take a moment to consider the following questions. Then, write your responses in the spaces provided.

1. *Find a vision for the future*

What do you think is important for you to accomplish during your youth/teenage years?

_____

_____

What dreams did you or do you have for yourself in upcoming days/weeks/months/years/life?

_____

_____

What are you here on the planet for?

_____

_____

In what area do you think you could you make a contribution?

_____

_____

What would you try to do with your life if you knew that you could not fail?

_____

_____

2. Deal with and dissolve barriers to the preferred future

What, in your view, stops you from getting to where you want to be with your life?

_____

_____

What, in your view, stops you from realizing your dreams or getting to your goals?

_____

_____

What do you believe must happen before you can realize your dreams/future?

_____

_____

What are the actions you haven't taken to make your dreams and visions come true?

_____

_____

What things stand in your way of realizing your dreams and visions?

_____

_____

What would your heroes, models, or people you admire do if they were you to make this dream or vision happen?

_____

_____

3. *Make an action plan to reach the preferred future*

What could you do in the near future that would move you toward getting you where you want to be?

_____

_____

What could you do in the near future that would move you toward realizing your visions and dreams?

_____

_____

What would be a first step toward realizing your dream/future?

_____

_____

What would you do as soon as you leave here?

_____

_____

What would you be thinking that would help you take those steps?

_____

_____

With most adolescents who are stuck in their troubles, just getting them to turn their gaze from the past to the future is a major reorientation. This reorientation can provide information about directions for treatment, meaning and purpose in their life, and lead to the restoration of hope.

PART III:
CHANGING THE DOING OF THE PROBLEM

36

Invitations to Accountability:
Separating Feeling and Doing

THERAPIST'S OVERVIEW

Purpose of Exercise

There are times when children and adolescents have difficulty distinguishing between what they experience internally (e.g., feelings, bodily sensations, etc.) and what they do behaviorally, through their actions and interactions. Often this blurring of boundaries leads children and adolescents to believe that because they feel a particular way it's OK to act in ways that are not appropriate.

The purpose of this exercise is to help children and adolescents to learn that while all of what they feel internally is acceptable, some actions are not. They are still accountable for their actions. This exercise can also help caregivers to distinguish between what their children and adolescents feel and how they behave. This exercise can be used at any point during therapy or with caregivers as a part of groups.

Suggestions for Use

1. This exercise is designed for use with parents.
2. Talk with clients about the differences between feelings and actions. Make sure that they understand the distinction between the two.
3. It can be helpful to first spend extra time with caregivers on the first part of the exercise, teaching them how to use statements that acknowledge and validate internal experience. If they are already adept at this, you may choose to go on to Part 2 right away.

EXERCISE

Part 1

Children and adolescents sometimes get the idea that what they feel inside is wrong, bad, or a problem. We want to let them know that whatever they feel inside is OK. It's not what people *feel* that causes problems; it's what they *do* as a result of those feelings that can be problematic. Therefore, the first thing that we want to do is acknowledge, validate, and give children and adolescents permission to feel whatever they feel.

Acknowledgement means that we hear what they are saying—the words that they use. The simplest way of conveying acknowledgement is to listen for feeling-oriented words such as hurt, sad, mad, angry, and so on, and repeat them back. For example, you could say, "You're sad" or "I heard you say that you're angry."

Validation means that we give permission for children and adolescents to feel the way they do. To validate internal experience, add "It's/that's okay" or "It's/that's all right" to the restatement of feeling. For example, you might say, "It's okay to be angry" or "It's all right if you're mad" or "I heard you say you're sad, and that's okay."

To complete Part 1 of this exercise, first read the child/adolescent response. Next, using acknowledgement and validation, write your own response in the spaces provided.

Examples

ADOLESCENT: "That really makes me mad!"
PARENT: "It's ok if you're mad."
CHILD: "I don't like doing homework."
PARENT: "It's all right to feel that way."

Adolescent: "I can't stand going to school."
Parent: _____

Adolescent: "That really pisses me off!"
Parent: _____

Child: "I miss my friends."
Parent: _____

Child: "Sometimes I don't want to go see Daddy."
Parent: _____

Part 2

We can help children and adolescents to distinguish between how they feel and what they do by paying attention to the way that we respond to their feelings and actions. To do this, we continue to use acknowledgement and validation for internal experience while simultaneously promoting accountability by calling attention to actions that are harmful to self or others or illegal.

To complete Part 2 of this exercise, first read the child/adolescent response. Next, in the spaces provided, use acknowledgement and validation and combine it with a statement inviting the child or adolescent to be accountable for his or her actions. One way to do this is to use the word "and" to separate internal experience from actions.

Examples

ADOLESCENT: "She made me so mad so I told her off."
PARENT: "It's ok to be mad at her and it's not ok to tell her off."

ADOLESCENT: "If someone did that to me, that person would pay."
PARENT: "It's ok if you're upset by things that happen to you and you're still responsible for what you do.
CHILD: "See, you hate me, that's why you make me go to my room."
PARENT: "It's ok if you're mad or upset and it's not ok to hit your sister. You need to go to your room."

Adolescent: "If he's gonna say stuff and make me mad then I'm gonna smack him."
Parent: _____

Adolescent: "No one can treat me that way. So I'm gonna get even."
Parent: _____

Child: "He wrecked my building so I knocked him down."
Parent: _____

Child: "She didn't play the game right so we kicked her out."
Parent: _____

37

Identifying Unhelpful Patterns

THERAPIST'S OVERVIEW

Purpose of Exercise

We all have routines and ways of doing things in our lives. Sometimes we are aware of these routines or *patterns*. Other times we have no idea that we are engaging in acts of repetition. Furthermore, patterns can and often do contribute to the maintenance of problems. That is, without an awareness of repetitive behavior, patterns can keep problems going. We refer to these as unhelpful patterns of action and interaction.

This exercise is designed to help therapists and parents to identify patterns that maintain problems. To do this, it's important that therapists recognize that problematic actions and interactions occur in *context*. They occur at certain times, in certain places, last for different lengths of time, and so on. To learn about these aspects of context we ask questions about "who," "what," "when," "where," and "how." We call these 4WH questions. They can help us to get a clearer idea of what needs to change and to determine the aspects of the context within which the patterns exist. Then, therapists can work with clients to change, alter, and disrupt those patterns.

Suggestions for Use

1. This exercise can be used with parents, adolescents, and children.
2. Patterns can be individualized (actions) or can occur between people (interactions). Look for both possibilities in the maintenance of problems.
3. It's important to get clear, observable descriptions of actions and interactions. To assist with this, it can be helpful to familiarize clients with action-talk.

EXERCISE

Problems do not occur in a vacuum. That is, they occur at certain times, in certain places, with certain people, and so on. To determine the most appropriate method for solving a problem, it's first important to explore the patterns surrounding it. This exercise will help you, either alone or with your therapist, to identify those unhelpful patterns. Once this has been done, a variety of methods can be used to change, alter, and disrupt those unhelpful patterns of action and interaction.

To complete this exercise, write down your answers in the spaces provided.

How often does the problem typically happen (once an hour, once a day, once a week)?

_____

_____

_____

_____

What is the usual timing (time of day, time of week, time of month, time of year) of the problem?

Examples: Only on weekends? At night? After school?

_____

_____

_____

_____

How long does the problem typically last?

Examples: Five minutes? An hour? A day?

_____

_____

_____

_____

Where does the problem typically happen?

Examples: In the family room? In the car? In English class?

_____

_____

_____

_____

What do you do when the problem is happening?

Examples: Raise your voice? Leave the room? Pound on the table?

_____

_____

_____

_____

Who is usually present when the problem is happening?

Examples: Siblings? Teachers? Friends?

_____

_____

_____

_____

What do others usually do or say when the problem is happening?

Examples: Blame you or someone else? Join in and argue? Give advice?

_____

_____

_____

_____

By now, you have some ideas about the patterns that surround the problem you're facing. Next, talk with your therapist or consider methods in this section of the book for changing, altering, and disrupting those unhelpful patterns of action and interaction.

38

Identifying Solution Keys by Changing Patterns

THERAPIST'S OVERVIEW

Purpose of Exercise

When parents are faced with problems with their children or adolescents they are often very good at describing the details of such problems. That is, when problems happen, what is going on during those times, and so on. However, there are also exceptions to problematic patterns that can go unnoticed. Exceptions are times when problems don't occur or occur to a lesser degree. By identifying these moments in time, parents, children, and adolescents can learn when they have influence over the problem.

This exercise is designed to help therapists and parents to identify exceptions to unhelpful patterns that have been maintaining problems. To do this, it's important that therapists recognize that actions and interactions occur in *context*. They occur at certain times, in certain places, last for different lengths of time, and so on. This exercise can assist in the identification of contexts in which problems are absent or minimized in their intensity. These represent solution keys.

Suggestions for Use

1. This exercise can be used with parents, adolescents, and children.
2. Patterns can be individualized (actions) or can occur between people (interactions). Look for both possibilities in exploring exceptions to problems.
3. It's important to get clear, observable descriptions of actions and interactions. To assist with this, it can be helpful to familiarize clients with action-talk.
4. This exercise can be combined with "Identifying Unhelpful Patterns."

EXERCISE

Although it can seem as if some problems happen all the time, that idea is a myth. That is, problems occur at certain times, in certain places, with certain people, and so on. On the other hand, they are absent or less intrusive at other times. There is a saying, "Problems don't occur twenty-four hours a day." This exercise will help you, either alone, with your family, or with your therapist, to identify situations or contexts when you have influence over the problem. This influence represents "solution keys." Solution keys can help you to change aspects of problem patterns and essentially "turn off" problems or even prevent them.

Note: If you've already completed the exercise, "Identifying Unhelpful Patterns," you may want to refer back to it as you complete this exercise.

To complete this exercise, write down your responses in the spaces provided. In thinking about your responses, consider that although it *seems* as if the problems you've been facing happen all the time, that's just an idea. Pay close attention to the problem situation and notice that sometimes it's not so intrusive. For example, consider that even though your son yells at you, he doesn't yell at his teachers. Or, your daughter gets poor grades in English but does well in math. These are exceptions.

When does the problem rarely happen or not at all?

Examples: Not on weekends. Never in the evenings. Rarely after lunch. Not when her friends are around.

_____

_____

_____

_____

_____

Where does the problem rarely happen or not at all?

Examples: Not at school. Never in the kitchen. Rarely in the car. Never at the grandparents' house.

_____

_____

_____

_____

_____

What constants are present when the problem doesn't seem to be happening or is happening less frequently?

Examples: If he ate breakfast then he usually has a good day. If she went to bed on time the night before things go better the next day.

_____

_____

_____

_____

_____

Who is present or not present when the problem isn't happening or is happening less? If present, what does that person(s) do to help? If not present, how does that help? (Be specific about words, body language, voicing, and actions.)

_____

_____

_____

_____

_____

What are you usually doing when the problem is less noticeable or absent altogether? (Be specific about words, body language, voicing, and actions.)

_____

_____

_____

_____

_____

By now you have some ideas about what is different about the times that you have some influence over the problem you've been up against. Next, consider deliberately doing or building on those things that seem to aid in alleviating the problem to any degree or in holding it completely at bay. You may also want to explore this further with your therapist.

39

Changing Patterns in Relationships

THERAPIST'S OVERVIEW

Purpose of Exercise

People become engaged in patterns—ways of acting and interacting with others. Some of these patterns work well, others don't. In the midst of problems, it's common for one person to wait for the other person to change in a way he or she prefers. This can keep people waiting for an eternity. Yet if the person desiring the change takes the initiative and does something different to change the relationship, positive change may come about more quickly.

The purpose of this exercise is to encourage parents, children, adolescents, and other family members to make small changes in their relationships. This can lead to problem resolution.

Suggestions for Use

1. This exercise can be used with parents, adolescents, and children.
2. This exercise can involve one person or several people each changing a pattern.
3. Remind clients that often only a small change is necessary to change a pattern. They do not need to make drastic changes.
4. Remind clients that if a particular change does not bring about the desired results, try something different.

EXERCISE

Sometimes people don't make an effort because they believe that "nobody will notice," that it won't make a difference, or that they don't believe it's their problem to change. Is that happening in your situation? Here is an experiment to see if making a change in a pattern will make a difference in your relationship with your child, adolescent, spouse, or significant other.

To complete this exercise, write your response to each inquiry on the spaces provided.

State a typical pattern that happens in your relationship that you would like to change. (A pattern is anything, positive or negative, that repeats itself. Patterns involve the actions of individuals and interactions between people. For example, a pattern might be that when your daughter becomes angry she yells. Then you yell at her in an effort to stop her from yelling. In response, she becomes louder and threatens to leave. Your response is to threaten her with grounding if she leaves.)

_____

_____

_____

_____

_____

Next, have each person involved in the pattern pick a way to change the pattern in a way that he or she thinks might improve the relationship. Each person ought to agree to do the new pattern three times in the next week. If you are the only one willing to try this exercise, then try it on your own.

After trying out your pattern for a week, write down the three instances when you acted differently.

1. _____

2. _____

3. _____

What difference did it make to change your actions involved in the pattern?

_____

_____

_____

_____

_____

Write down the three things the other person did differently when you changed your actions involved in the pattern.

1. _____

2. _____

3. _____

After the other person responded to your changes in the pattern, how did you respond?

1. _____

2. _____

3. _____

In the end, how did changing the pattern change your relationship?

_____

_____

_____

_____

_____

What does this tell you about yourself? About the other person? About the two of you together?

_____

_____

_____

_____

_____

40

Go with the Pattern

THERAPIST'S OVERVIEW

Purpose of Exercise

Often, parents, adolescents, and children will complain of the interaction that "happens everyday." They find themselves in an unsatisfying pattern but feel helpless to break out of it. Frequently, if you suggest a change, they will explain that they have already tried that or they know that it won't work. The purpose of this exercise is to join with the client in their problem pattern and at the same time make it difficult for the pattern to continue. Rather than trying to convince them to solve the problem your way, you might explain that since the solution hasn't presented itself yet, it might be helpful to study the interaction in more detail by purposefully repeating it. This suggests that they replace something that feels automatic with purposeful and deliberate action. Clients will likely have difficulty carrying out this exercise, but if that is the case, they will have broken the pattern. If they are able to successfully repeat the pattern, you can talk about that experience. Focusing on the difficulties they had reproducing the pattern implies that it takes effort to preserve the status quo. As a result, they may be able to identify parts of the interaction where they do, in fact, have control.

Suggestions for Use

1. This exercise can be used with parents, adolescents, and children.
2. The first part of this exercise can be completed in this session.
3. You may want to be more specific in suggesting the frequency and timing for doing the exercise.
4. In reviewing the exercise with your clients, you may want to ask them how they knew it was time to end the exercise.

EXERCISE

Some patterns of behavior can be extremely stubborn when you try to change them with pure will power. When a car is stuck in snow or mud you must rock it back and forth, momentarily going backwards, before you can get out of the rut. This exercise may help you do the same thing with your relationship. Sometimes it is helpful to "go with" the problem behavior and study it before you can find a way to change it.

To complete this exercise, write down your answers in the spaces provided.

Write a step-by-step description of the typical problematic interaction involving your child or adolescent. Be very specific about who says and does what and at what time. Be sure you leave no doubt about each person's lines. Use another piece of paper if necessary.

_____

_____

_____

_____

_____

_____

_____

_____

_____

Become familiar with your role in the interaction.

Next, between now and your next session, anytime you feel that the pattern is beginning, let the others know that it is time for you all to repeat the pattern. Play your role and repeat the pattern as you have in the past. If someone who typically is involved in the interaction refuses to participate, willing members of the family can still perform their roles.

Each time you do this, answer the following questions, making notes as necessary so you can discuss your experience in the next session. In addition, rate yourself on your performance, that is, how well you followed your script. Use a scoring method of your choice.

What was the hardest thing about playing your role, as written?

_____

_____

_____

_____

At what point were you tempted to step out of your script and improvise something different?

_____

_____

If so, how did you resist that temptation?

_____

_____

_____

_____

_____

If you were tempted, what did you consider doing differently?

_____

_____

_____

_____

As a result of this exercise, what did you notice and/or learn about the problematic pattern?

_____

_____

_____

_____

_____

41

On and Off

THERAPIST'S OVERVIEW

Purpose of the Exercise

Sometimes, parents and children or adolescents get into a war of wills that makes it difficult for one to do something different without losing face. The purpose of this exercise is to offer a way for clients to experiment with new behavior without committing to long-term change.

Suggestions for Use

1. This exercise is mainly for parents but can also be used with adolescents.
2. This exercise can be presented as an opportunity to experiment with new behaviors and then decide later if the client wants to continue them.
3. If is often helpful for both parties to identify new behaviors they will experiment with.
4. An advantage of this exercise is that it requires the client to make an effort only half the time.

Note: It can be helpful to orient the client to action-talk. You can either discuss it with them or have them complete the exercise, "The Language of Change: Using Action-Talk," prior to this exercise.

EXERCISE

Sometimes, parents get into patterns of behavior that don't work for them but they don't know how to break out of them. This is an exercise to help you experiment with something different to see if you want to continue it. Often, this kind of experimentation is helpful in trying to be creative and thinking out of the box with children and adolescents.

To complete this exercise, on the rest of this page write a description of the way you "do" the problem. Be specific about what each person does and says and use action-talk if you prefer.

_____

_____

_____

_____

_____

_____

_____

_____

_____

_____

_____

_____

_____

_____

_____

Next, on alternating days, starting today, do the problem behavior (e.g., a way that you often try to get your child or adolescent to do something that doesn't work) one day and not on the next. Then, answer the following questions before your next session.

On the days when you didn't do the problem, what did you do instead?

_____

_____

_____

_____

_____

Which do you prefer, the days you did the problem or the days when you didn't? Why?

_____

_____

_____

_____

_____

_____

_____

_____

_____

_____

_____

What did you learn from completing this exercise? What might you do differently as a result?

_____

_____

_____

_____

Bring this completed exercise to your next session if you are currently in therapy.

42

Do Something Different

THERAPIST'S OVERVIEW

Purpose of Exercise

When people become stuck it's often because they are repeating patterns of action and inter-action that maintain problems. In such cases, it can be helpful to work with clients to identify unhelpful patterns and search for small areas where these patterns can be interrupted, altered, or changed in some way. The purpose of this exercise is to help parents to make small changes in their actions and interactions to change problematic patterns with children and adolescents.

Suggestions for Use

1. This exercise is designed to be used with parents.
2. It's generally a good idea to suggest that parents make small changes as opposed to trying to do a complete overhaul. A small change is often all that is necessary to break up unhelp-ful patterns.
3. Be sure that whatever clients intend to do different is "doable." That is, it won't be hard to undertake and will not require major changes in lifestyle. Changes in patterns that are do-able and not too difficult have a better chance of being utilized on a regular or ongoing ba-sis.

Note: This exercise can be used with "Identifying Unhelpful Patterns."

EXERCISE

We all repeat patterns in our lives. Sometimes our personal patterns of action and interaction keep problems going instead of bringing them to an end. This exercise is designed to help you change patterns in your relationships with your children and adolescents.

To complete this exercise, write your response to each inquiry on the spaces provided.

State a typical pattern that happens in your relationship that you would like to change. (A pattern is anything, positive or negative, that repeats itself. Patterns involve the actions of individuals and interactions between people. For example, a pattern might be that when your daughter be-comes angry she yells. Then you yell at her in an effort to stop her from yelling. In response, she becomes louder and threatens to leave. Your response is to threaten her with grounding if she leaves.)

_____

_____

_____

_____

Next, have each person involved in the pattern pick a way to change the pattern in a way that he or she thinks might improve the relationship. Each person ought to agree to do the new pattern three times in the next week. If you are the only one willing to try this exercise, then try it on your own.

After trying out your pattern for a week, write down the three instances when you acted differently.

1. _____

2. _____

3. _____

What difference did it make to change your actions involved in the pattern?

_____

_____

_____

_____

Write down the three things the other person did differently when you changed your actions involved in the pattern.

1. _____

2. _____

3. _____

After the other person responded to your changes in the pattern, how did you respond?

_____

_____

_____

_____

In the end, how did changing the pattern change the problem you were facing?

_____

_____

_____

_____

What does this tell you about yourself? About the other person(s) involved? About the two/three of you together?

_____

_____

_____

_____

43

The Unified Front

THERAPIST'S OVERVIEW

Purpose of Exercise

There isn't always a consensus among parents about how to set and enforce rules and create and deliver consequences. However, if there is a lack of a "unified front" between parents, children and adolescents are likely to find this out. They can then learn to "work the system" to get the outcome they want.

The purpose of this exercise is to help parents work together to create and follow through with such issues as rules and consequences. This can allow things to go smoother at home and lessen the stress in family relationships.

Suggestions for Use

1. This exercise is designed for use with parents and can be completed during a counseling session or between sessions.
2. It's often a good idea to reorient parents to times in the past when they have been able to work things out. For example, a therapist might say, "Tell me about a time when you were able to come to an agreement about some difficult issue. How did you do that?" This can prime them for this exercise.
3. Encourage parents to create rules that are realistic and developmentally appropriate for the ages of their children and adolescents. In addition, suggest that there are some rules that are negotiable and some that are not. With the rules that are negotiable, encourage parents to find a way of including their sons and daughters in developing them.
4. After agreeing on rules, encourage parents to share the rules with their children and adolescents together, thereby demonstrating a united front.

EXERCISE

It's hard to agree on everything. Yet one particular area that can cause friction in families is when parents don't agree with each other on rules and consequences. Ironically, children and adolescents have an uncanny way of finding out when there are disagreements and in finding out what it takes to turn the tables in their favor. This can undermine the efforts of one or both parents in trying to maintain some sense of structure. It can also cause marital friction and discord. The purpose of this exercise is to help the parental team work together to develop rules and consequences for their children and adolescents.

To complete this exercise, write your response to each question in the spaces provided.

What are the rules and consequences that you frequently disagree about? List each one.

1. _____

2. _____

3. _____

4. _____

5. _____

6. _____

7. _____

8. _____

9. _____

10. _____

In the past, when you've had some form of disagreement (about anything), how did it get worked out? What did each of you do to contribute to its resolution?

_____

_____

_____

_____

_____

_____

_____

_____

What are some early signs that would let you know that a disagreement is brewing about the rules or consequences?

1. _____

2. _____

3. _____

4. _____

5. _____

The next time either of you notice a disagreement starting, inform your children or adolescents that you are going into a conference to discuss the matter. Do your best to find a quiet place to talk about the rules or consequences. In addition, try not to be pressured to make any quick decisions that you might later undo. This will only undermine one or both of you in the eyes of your sons and daughters.

When you are finished, log the results of your discussion in the spaces provided.

_____

_____

_____

_____

_____

_____

_____

_____

_____

If you think that a change in rules is called for, be sure to set time to discuss this change of rules. Try to find a quiet place and time, and allot enough time to find a mutual agreement.

Bear in mind that with some rules you may want to include the rest of the family. This can help with relationship building.

When delivering rules and consequences, as much as possible, try to deliver them together. When this is not possible, at least be sure that there is agreement about the outcome. Remember that oftentimes what creates the most effect is not the consequence itself, but the waiting between the violation and the delivery of the consequence. So don't feel pressured to come up with something quickly just to get it over with. Give your children and adolescents time to reflect on their behavior.

44

Change Some Aspect of Context

THERAPIST'S OVERVIEW

Purpose of Exercise

Problems occur at certain times, in certain places, last for different lengths of time, and so on. This also means that there are times, places, and so on when problems do not occur. Whether it's time, location, or some other aspect, all of these things are part of what we refer to as context. We've learned that changing any one aspect of context can lead to the resolution of a problem. This exercise is designed to help parents make small changes involving some aspect of context, which can lead to problem resolution.

Suggestions for Use

1. This exercise is designed for use with parents.
2. It's generally a good idea to suggest that parents make small changes as opposed to trying to do a complete overhaul. A small change is often all that is necessary to break up unhelpful patterns.
3. Be sure that whatever clients intend to do different is "doable." That is, it won't be hard to undertake and will not require major changes in lifestyle. Changes that are doable and not too difficult for clients have a better chance of being continued on a regular or ongoing basis.

Note: This exercise is best paired with "Identifying Unhelpful Patterns" and "Identifying Solution Keys by Changing Patterns."

EXERCISE

Take a moment to consider that problems occur in context. That is, they take place at certain times, in certain places, and in certain situations. On the other hand, there are times, places, and situations when they do not occur. This exercise can help you to make small changes in a number of areas that can ultimately lead to the resolution of the problem you're facing with your son or daughter.

Note: Although this exercise can be completed independently, we've found it helpful to first complete the exercise "Identifying Unhelpful Patterns."

To complete this exercise, review the different aspects of context that are listed as follows. Consider which one, two, or three you believe apply to the problem you've been facing. Then, write your response to each inquiry on the spaces provided.

Notice the usual timing of the problem—when it happens, how long it lasts, or the frequency. Next, make a small change in the timing. For example, if your son argues with you after dinner and before he is supposed to do his homework, begin the arguing before dinner. Or, if two of your children refuse to do their chores, tell them that they can refuse if they want, but that they must verbally refuse for no less than fifteen minutes. Record how you changed the timing and the results in the spaces provided.

Notice the usual location of the problem or the spatial arrangements of it (e.g., where it occurs, the distance between you and your son/daughter when you argue, etc.). Next, change the location or spatial arrangement. For example, if your son argues with you in the kitchen, move the argument into the garage or completely outside. Record how you changed the location or spatial arrangement and the results in the spaces provided.

Identify your usual way of relating to your child or adolescent. Pay close attention to your voice tone, the words you use, and your nonverbal behaviors. Next, make a small change in your pattern of relating. For example, if you typically stand up with your arms folded and use a stern voice when giving your child/adolescent a consequence, consider sitting down, relaxing your arms, and using a calm voice. Remember that often, only one or two small changes are necessary. Record how you changed your way of relating and the results in the spaces provided.

Now that you have completed this exercise, select one aspect of context and during the next week make the change that you wrote down. Be sure to track how it works for you and what results you attain. If changing one aspect of context does not bring about the results you were seeking, try modifying your idea or changing another aspect.

45

Something Different, Something New, Something Unpredictable, Something Else to Do

THERAPIST'S OVERVIEW

Purpose of Exercise

It's very easy for parents to get stuck in patterns of action and interaction that are part of the problem. Although these are typically parents' best efforts, they actually play a role in maintaining the problem. In effect, the solution to the problem becomes the problem. This exercise offers parents multiple ways of changing problematic patterns of action and interaction through simple yet effective means.

Suggestions for Use

1. This exercise is designed for use with parents.
2. It's generally a good idea to suggest that parents make small changes as opposed to trying to do a complete overhaul. A small change is often all that is necessary to break unhelpful patterns.
3. Be sure that whatever clients intend to do different is "doable." That is, it won't be hard to undertake and will not require major changes in lifestyle. Changes that are doable and not too difficult for clients have a better chance of being continued on a regular or ongoing basis.
4. Although it can be helpful to offer parents ideas for changing patterns, it's often more effective to elicit their ideas about what might work prior to doing so. Clients are more likely to use ideas that they have some investment in and helped develop.

Note: This exercise is best paired with "Identifying Unhelpful Patterns" and "Identifying Solution Keys by Changing Patterns."

EXERCISE

There's an old saying, "Insanity is doing the same thing over and over and expecting different results." Despite this, we all find ourselves repeating patterns that we believe will bring about problem resolution, only to find that nothing has changed. In some instances, our attempts at solution actually keep the problem going and sometimes make it worse. This exercise will help you to change those patterns that you sometimes replicate with your child or adolescent. It's important that you use your creativity with this exercise. In addition, bear in mind that if something doesn't bring about the results you desire, try something else.

Note: Although this exercise can be completed independently, we've found it helpful to first complete the exercise "Identifying Unhelpful Patterns."

To complete this exercise, be sure that you are clear on the problem that you want to see change. Next, review the different ways of changing patterns. Then, choose one or two that you believe might work with your situation. Last, write your response to each inquiry on the spaces provided.

Interrupt or prevent the occurrence of the problem. For example, before your daughter has the chance to refuse doing her homework, beat her to the punch by saying, "I bet you're going to refuse to do your homework." Or, with the same example, if your daughter refuses, put her books away and leave the room, thereby preventing the argument that usually follows with her. Record how you interrupted or prevented the occurrence of the problem and the results in the spaces provided.

_____

_____

_____

_____

_____

Add a new element to the problem. For example, if your son uses profanity or calls you names when addressing you, make him aware of what you are doing and use a small hand-held tape recorder to tape his tirades. Or, with the same problem, contact your spouse or significant other, a teacher, friend, or some other person so that they can listen in on the tirade. Record how you added a new element to the problem and the results in the spaces provided.

_____

_____

_____

_____

_____

Break up the problem into smaller elements. For example, if you and your significant other argue each time you try to discuss how to discipline your child, get a timer and allow one person to speak for two minutes. Then, reset the timer and let the other person speak for the same amount of time. Do this until the issue is resolved. Or, if your adolescent refuses to do his or her chores, chart out each chore and assign them one at a time. Record how you broke up the problem into smaller elements and the results in the spaces provided.

_____

_____

_____

_____

_____

Create an ordeal by linking the problem pattern with some burdensome activity. For example, if your adolescent is truant from school and is missing out on his or her education, each evening following a day that he or she has skipped, sit and read to him and become the educator. Or, with an adolescent who refuses to do homework, have him or her sit with you and listen to classical music (or music he or she can't stand) during homework time. Record how you created an ordeal and the results in the spaces provided.

_____

_____

_____

_____

_____

Now that you have completed this exercise, select one method of changing an unwanted pattern. Be sure to track how it works for you and what results you attain. If one method does not bring about the results you were seeking, try modifying your idea or doing something else.

46

Follow the Script

THERAPIST'S OVERVIEW

Purpose of the Exercise

Parents often experience problems with their children and adolescents as being out of their control. This exercise attempts to provide a way for the therapist to join with parents to offer a way for them to begin to take some control. Suggesting that a parent willingly do something that has been experienced as out of control puts him or her in a position of either doing the pattern willfully or doing something different. In either case, something has changed. This can be especially helpful with parents who have the perspective that things are "out of control" or that they have "no control" regarding their children or adolescents.

Suggestions for Use

1. This exercise is designed for use with parents.
2. If the parent repeats the pattern, explore any difficulty or effort that may have been encountered in doing so.
3. Explore any deviation from the script in detail.
4. If a new pattern or behavior emerges, explore the possible benefits of it.
5. You may want to introduce the exercise as a way of helping the parent explore the problem pattern in more detail.
6. It might be helpful to write the script in the session.

EXERCISE

Problems often seem to take on familiar patterns. You may think of them as ruts that you are stuck in. Just as spinning your wheels often won't get you out of the mud, pushing ahead often just seems to dig you deeper in the rut. You may have learned that you sometimes need to put the car in reverse momentarily and "rock" the car back and forth to get out of a muddy rut. This exercise offers a way for you to do something similar with the problem you've been facing with your child or adolescent.

To complete this exercise, on this page, write a script for the way you usually do the problem. Write it so that someone reading it could fill in for one of the persons involved. Then, any time the problem begins to happen, follow the script as it is written. Before your next session, answer the questions that follow.

_____

_____

_____

_____

_____

_____

_____

_____

_____

_____

_____

_____

_____

_____

_____

_____

What difficulties did you encounter in carrying out the exercise?

1. _____

2. _____

3. _____

When were you tempted to ad lib and how did you stop yourself?

1. _____

2. _____

3. _____

What changes would you like to make to your part of the script?

1. _____

2. _____

3. _____

How has this affected your view of the problem?

1. _____

2. _____

3. _____

47

Identifying and Utilizing Past Solutions and Successes

THERAPIST'S OVERVIEW

Purpose of Exercise

In the midst of chaos, problems can mask the influence that parents, children, and adolescents have over them. Furthermore, therapists can become convinced that problems are pervasive and too difficult for their clients to overcome. Yet we know that problems vary in intensity. They vacillate on a continuum from being extremely dominating to having little influence. In addition, there are times when parents haven't experienced the problem full force, or expected to experience the problem but it didn't happen. There are times in the past when parents, children, and adolescents have had some influence over their problems.

This exercise is designed to help therapists, parents, children, and adolescents to identify past solutions and successes in regard to current problems. Once the influences over the problem have been identified, clients can determine what it will take to bring them into the present tense and do them more deliberately.

Suggestions for Use

1. This exercise is designed for use with parents, adolescents, or children.
2. In searching for past solutions and successes, it is important that therapists work to identify small influences that clients have had over problems. For example, a therapist wouldn't say, "When didn't you have the problem?" That can be invalidating to people and may garner a response of, "I always have the problem." Instead, a therapist might say, "Tell me about a time when the problem could have overwhelmed you but it didn't."
3. Have clients be as specific as possible about what they have done in the past that has worked to any degree. Action-talk can be helpful in gaining clear, observable descriptions.
4. This exercise can be combined with "Identifying Unhelpful Patterns."

EXERCISE

When facing problems with children and adolescents it can seem as if things are "always" going poorly and will "never" change. Even though problems vary in intensity, in the midst of difficulty, it can seem as though nothing works or ever will work. This exercise will help you to identify times when you had some influence over the problem. This includes times when the problem was happening but it didn't have the usual impact, and times when you expected the problem to happen but it didn't. These represent exceptions to the problem pattern, including past solutions and partial solutions/successes.

Note: If you've already completed the exercise, "Identifying Unhelpful Patterns," you may want to refer back to it as you complete this exercise.

To complete this exercise, write down your responses in the spaces provided.

Think about your experience with the problem. Recall a time when the problem happened and you were able to get somewhat of a handle on it and it didn't overwhelm you as it usually does. What specifically happened?

_____

_____

_____

_____

_____

What was different about the time that you were able to have some influence over the problem? What did you do? (Be specific about words, body language, voicing, and actions.) How was that different from what you usually do?

_____

_____

_____

_____

_____

Who else, if anyone, was present during that time? What did that person(s) do?

_____

_____

_____

_____

_____

What does your experience with having some influence over the problem tell you about your-self? About your son or daughter? About the problem?

_____

_____

_____

_____

_____

By now, you have some ideas about what is different about the times that you, your child, or adolescent has had some influence over the problem. Next, consider deliberately doing or building on those things that seem to aid in alleviating the problem to any degree or in holding it completely at bay. You may also want to explore this further with your therapist.

48

How Does the Problem End or Start to End?

Purpose of Exercise

The problems that parents experience with children and adolescents have end points. Solution patterns exist. This exercise is designed to help therapists, parents, children, and adolescents identify specific actions, interactions, and patterns that assist in bringing problems to an end. Once these influences over the problem have been identified, clients can determine what it will take to bring them into the present tense and do them more deliberately.

Suggestions for Use

1. This exercise can be used with parents, adolescents, and children.
2. It can be helpful to explore with clients multiple occasions when the problem happened and learn what brought the problem to an end each time. There may be multiple variations of "what worked," some of which will be useful and some of which will not.
3. Have clients be as specific as possible about what they or others have done to bring the problem to an end. Action-talk can be helpful in gaining clear, observable descriptions.
4. This exercise can be combined with "Identifying Unhelpful Patterns."

EXERCISE

Even though it doesn't seem that way, the problems that you've faced in the past did come to an end, if only for a short while. By exploring what brings problems to an end, it may be possible to identify specific things that you could do earlier on rather than letting the problem overwhelm you for extended periods of time. This exercise will assist you in determining the details of how problems are brought to an end in your life.

Note: If you've already completed the exercise, "Identifying Unhelpful Patterns," you may want to refer back to it as you complete this exercise.

To complete this exercise, write down your responses in the spaces provided.

Think about your experience with a specific problem that you've been facing. How does that problem typically end? Be as specific as possible.

_____

_____

_____

_____

_____

How do you know when the problem is coming to an end? How do you know that it's beginning to wind down? What's the first thing that you notice?

_____

_____

_____

_____

_____

How can others tell when the problem has subsided or started to subside?

_____

_____

_____

_____

_____

What do you or others do that helps to bring the problem to an end? (Be specific about words, body language, voicing, and actions.)

_____

_____

_____

_____

_____

By now, you have some ideas about what it is that you, your child, adolescent, or others do to bring the problem you've been facing to an end. You may even have multiple ideas. Now consider how you might use what you've learned earlier on, once the problem has surfaced, as opposed to letting it run its full course. You may be able to short circuit the problem right away. You may also want to explore this further with your therapist.

49

How Come Things Haven't Bottomed Out?

THERAPIST'S OVERVIEW

Purpose of Exercise

When situations don't seem to be improving, it can be helpful to have parents, children, or adolescents speculate as to why things aren't *worse*. This can be especially helpful when, as a therapist, your attempts to help don't seem to be producing the results that clients are seeking. Once those resilient qualities and actions that have kept things from "bottoming out" have been identified, therapists can help clients to build on them and perhaps change the direction of change. This exercise can help clinicians and clients acknowledge the difficulties being faced while simultaneously searching for those qualities and actions that keep people afloat.

Suggestions for Use

1. This exercise is designed for use with parents and adolescents.
2. It's important that therapists acknowledge the pain and suffering that clients are experiencing prior to inquiring about why the problem isn't worse. For example, a therapist might say, "You've certainly been through a lot and it seems like things just aren't getting any better. In fact, to you it seems like they're getting worse. I'm curious, how have you kept things from completely bottoming out?"
3. When clients respond with vague answers such as "We love each other" or "We can't give up" be sure to find out what that allows them to do. For example, a therapist might inquire, "What has the love that you have for each other allowed you to do to keep things from going downhill further?" Have clients be as specific as possible about what they or others have done to keep things from getting worse. Action-talk can be helpful in gaining clear, observable descriptions.
4. This exercise can be combined with "Identifying Unhelpful Patterns."

EXERCISE

When problems don't seem to be getting any better and in fact, seem to be getting worse, it's important to remember that more often than not, things *can get even worse*. Despite this, many families have unique qualities and have taken action to keep things from "bottoming out." This exercise is designed to help you identify those qualities that exist within yourself, your child or adolescent, and/or within your family system that have kept the problem you've been facing from completely taking over and sinking the family ship.

To complete this exercise, write down your responses in the spaces provided.

Think about your experience with a specific problem that you've been facing. How come things haven't completely bottomed out?

_____

_____

_____

_____

_____

What specific action have you taken to prevent things from bottoming out? Be as specific as possible.

_____

_____

_____

_____

_____

Despite all that you've been through, how have you or others managed to take steps to keep things from deteriorating further?

_____

_____

_____

_____

_____

What have others done to prevent things from bottoming out? (Be specific about words, body language, voicing, and actions.)

_____

_____

_____

_____

_____

What does your and other family members' ability to prevent things from deteriorating further say about you and others individually, and your family as a whole? How is it helpful for you to know that?

_____

_____

_____

_____

_____

By now, you have some ideas about what it is that you, your child, adolescent, others, or your family as a whole do to keep things from bottoming out. You may even have multiple ideas. Now consider how you might use what you've learned and build on it. This may help you to turn things around and get change going in the direction of problem resolution. You may also want to explore this further with your therapist.

– 50 –

Tracking Solutions

THERAPIST'S OVERVIEW

Purpose of the Exercise

This exercise invites the client to track progress quantitatively, visually, and graphically. It makes the subtle suggestion that there will be some days that are not as good as others and that perfection is unrealistic. It also provides ways of teaching the client to use his or her own perceptions to guide future efforts. This can be especially helpful with parents, children, and adolescents as it can help them to track progress toward goals.

Suggestions for Use

1. This exercise can be used individually with any family member or with an entire family.
2. Invite the client to choose a number between 1 and 10 that represents his or her experience of the problem on an average day.
3. Invite the client to choose a number to serve as a goal. Later, this number can provide guidance on knowing when to terminate work on the goal.
4. Explore the details of what was going on when the client's experience was better than the average day number stated at the start of therapy.
5. If there is no sign of improvement after several sessions, try something different.
6. You may want to use this exercise with all family members and track their responses on a single graph.

EXERCISE

You have experienced the fact that your problems change from day to day and that some days are better than others. Finding out what makes things better can be very helpful in deciding how you want to change your behavior. This exercise is designed to help you become more aware of what's different when things aren't so bad.

To complete this exercise, imagine your experience of the problem on a 1 to 10 scale. That is, 1 represents the worst the problem could make you feel and 10 represents the problem being completely gone. Once a day, look back over the past twenty-four hours and rate your day on this 1 to 10 scale. On the lines provided following the graph, write what you did that day that helped you deal with the problem. Bring this paper with you the next time you see your therapist.

Rating	Day 1	Day 2	Day 3	Day 4	Day 5	Day 6	Day 7
10							
9							
8							
7							
6							
5							
4							
3							
2							
1							

Day 1

_____

_____

_____

_____

_____

Day 2

_____

_____

_____

_____

_____

Day 3

_____

_____

_____

_____

_____

Day 4

_____

_____

_____

_____

Day 5

_____

_____

_____

_____

Day 6

_____

_____

_____

_____

Day 7

_____

_____

_____

_____

– 51 –

What Do You Do Well?

THERAPIST'S OVERVIEW

Purpose of Exercise

In the midst of problems with their children and adolescents, parents will often forget about the abilities that they have within themselves and their social systems. The purpose of this exercise is to help parents identify skills they already possess that may be helpful in resolving the concerns that they are experiencing with their children or adolescents. Once skills or abilities are identified, clients can be encouraged to explore how they can be helpful with the problems they are currently experiencing.

Suggestions for Use

1. This exercise is designed for use with parents.
2. It's important that clinicians acknowledge the difficulties that clients are experiencing before identifying what they do well. If this does not occur, it's unlikely that clients will feel that clinicians understand the severity of their problems, or, are giving short shrift to them.
3. Once clients identify what they do well, it's important to help them link those things with the problem context. To do this we ask, "How can being good at _____ be helpful with the problem that you're facing?" By doing this, clients can make meaningful connections as opposed to clinicians suggesting them.
4. This exercise can be used with parents, children, and adolescents—individually or together.

EXERCISE

We all have abilities and skills in certain areas of our lives. However, when we are experiencing problems with our children we often develop amnesia to those abilities and skills. That is, we forget them. This exercise will help you identify the abilities and skills that accompany the things that you do well. In turn, these skills can be helpful in resolving the problems you've been facing.

To complete this exercise, first identify and write down ten things that you do well. Be creative. Then, for each thing that you do well, write down three skills that are involved with it.

1. What I do well

_____

_____

Skills: _____

_____

_____

2. What I do well

_____

_____

Skills: _____

_____

_____

3. What I do well

_____

_____

Skills: _____

_____

_____

4. What I do well

_____

_____

Skills: _____

_____

_____

5. What I do well

_____

_____

Skills: _____

_____

_____

6. What I do well

_____

_____

Skills: _____

_____

_____

7. What I do well

_____

_____

Skills: _____

_____

_____

8. What I do well

_____

_____

Skills: _____

_____

_____

9. What I do well

_____

_____

Skills: _____

_____

_____

10. What I do well

_____

_____

Skills: _____

_____

_____

Take some time to reflect on what you do well and the skills and abilities that are associated with those things. What did you learn about yourself?

For Parents

How might you use those abilities to help you with the problem that you've been facing with your son or daughter?

For Children/Adolescents

How might you use those abilities to help you with the problem that you've been facing?

52

What Worked?

THERAPIST'S OVERVIEW

Purpose of the Exercise

In therapy, clients can learn to apply their skills and abilities to solve their problems. Therefore, it makes sense to clarify what has happened and what resources clients have utilized that made success possible. By doing this, parents and adolescents can learn to use them more deliberately in the future if problems arise again. In addition, their views of themselves often change to seeing themselves as more confident when they have success. The purpose of this exercise is to bring this to the attention of parents and adolescents. Giving them a way to access all this information in the future can be helpful.

Suggestions for Use

1. This exercise is designed for use with parents and adolescents.
2. Suggest this exercise near the end of therapy.
3. Discuss the client's responses and suggest that this information may be helpful in dealing with similar problems in the future.
4. Take opportunities to emphasize the client's competency.

EXERCISE

Reaching your goals is an important accomplishment. But wait. There's even better news. You have learned things from this experience that you can apply to future challenges. This exercise will help you to identify what you did to accomplish your goal(s), the resources you used, and how you might use them in the future should you be faced with the same or a different problem.

To complete this exercise, fill in your responses in the spaces provided.

What did you do or not do that helped you? What specific actions did you take?

_____

_____

_____

_____

What was the first thing you noticed that indicated to you that you were making progress?

_____

_____

_____

_____

What did your therapist do or not do that was helpful?

_____

_____

_____

_____

List three things you learned from therapy:

1. _____

2. _____

3. _____

What does your success say about you?

_____

_____

_____

_____

How can what you learned help you to face the same or different problems in the future?

_____

_____

_____

_____

Store this where you can find it if you need it in the future.

53

Parents' 911

THERAPIST'S OVERVIEW

Purpose of the Exercise

In therapy, parents often have plans and ideas in their sessions but find them difficult to implement under the demands of everyday life. Preparing parents for these circumstances can be helpful. This exercise offers a way for parents to, in effect, take the session with them and step back into it when they most need to.

Suggestions for Use

1. This exercise is designed for use with parents.
2. Acknowledge the difficulty of changing old habits.
3. In the session, encourage the client to identify how he or she will know that it is time to refer to this exercise.
4. In the session, invite the client to identify a location to store this exercise so it will be available when needed.
5. Offer to make extra copies so one is always available.

EXERCISE

No matter how skillful you become at parenting, situations sometimes get the better of you. During the times when stress makes it hard to be creative, it sometimes helps to have a plan for getting back on track. This exercise will help you to think about what to do when the heat is on. We'll also give you suggestions to consider at the end of the exercise.

While it is relatively calm, think about your role as a parent. Next, list some of the qualities of the kind of parent you want to be.

1. _____

2. _____

3. _____

4. _____

5. _____

Set goals for both the long- and short-term future. Make them clear and precise.

1. _____

2. _____

3. _____

4. _____

5. _____

Keep track of the things that work. On good days, what is different? In particular, what do you do that seems to help? Write them down so you don't forget.

_____

_____

_____

_____

_____

When things aren't going so well:

1. Think of your role as that of teacher. If there has been a failure, it can mean simply that this is an area where you need to focus. What will be your lesson plan?
2. Do something different. Think about what you normally do in this situation. If it doesn't work, try something else.
3. You might do something entirely new or perhaps change an old pattern.
4. Consider delaying action. If you are too emotional to think clearly, you might want to say something like, "I'm too upset to deal with you now. Go to your room until I can calm down, then I will give you your consequences."
5. Remember that you are the parent. You don't have to justify your decisions to your children. Many things need to happen just because you are in charge and you've decided how things need to be. You may decide that you don't have to make everyone happy.
6. Ask for help. If there is a partner around, get him or her to take over before you lose it. If you are stuck, it may be time to talk with a counselor.
7. Pick your battles. You can't teach every lesson every day. Decide what is the most important thing for your child to learn at this time. If something isn't high priority, you might want to save it for another day. Keep perspective.
8. Learn to forgive yourself. You are learning, too. Nobody ever raised your child before.
9. Add your own ideas as they occur to you. They will probably be the best for you.

Keep this sheet handy so you can find it any time you need it.

54

How About a Ritual?

THERAPIST'S OVERVIEW

Purpose of Exercise

Growing up, many families had specific dinner times, certain meals on certain days, movie nights, and so on. All of these, as well as other family-oriented events, represent rituals. Rituals are those activities that occur daily, weekly, monthly, seasonally, and yearly. Essentially, rituals provide consistency in the lives of children and adolescents. In fact, research has demonstrated that children who come from homes where there has been abuse, alcoholism, divorce, or some other disruption or trauma tend to do better as adults when their rituals are kept intact or new rituals are put in place.

The purpose of this exercise is to help families in which there has been trauma, turmoil, or disruption to move through these times by maintaining old rituals or beginning new ones. This can provide consistency and comfort for children and adolescents.

Suggestions for Use

1. Rituals can occur with a few people or entire families. For example, a ritual may be that a particular parent always drives a particular teenager to baseball practice. A ritual for an entire family may be watching a particular television show on a particular night each week.
2. Sometimes parents will say that they do their rituals but their children don't seem interested, don't care, or won't be involved. Encourage them to involve their children and adolescents in conversations about family rituals. In addition, even though it may *seem* that their children and adolescents are uninterested, let parents know that they often are interested and just don't show it until a later age. What is important is that the rituals continue. This way, children and adolescents know they are happening and can count on them when needed.
3. Rituals can be those that are already in place. They can be old rituals that were disrupted due to some change in the family, or, they can be completely new ones.

EXERCISE

When we think of the past, we often recall consistent things that happened in our lives. For example, we may recall having dinner at the same time each evening, or going to the park every Saturday during the summer. Another event might have been family night when everyone went out for pizza and a movie. Those consistent happenings in our lives are often referred to as rituals. Rituals can help to bring consistency and stability to the lives of children and adolescents and to family relationships. They can occur daily, weekly, monthly, seasonally, and yearly. This exercise will help you to identify your current rituals and perhaps think of ways of establishing new ones.

To complete this exercise, write your responses to the questions in the spaces provided.

What are the current rituals that your family has in place? You may want to think of rituals as routine things that happen on a very regular basis. List each one.

1. _____

2. _____

3. _____

4. _____

5. _____

6. _____

7. _____

8. _____

9. _____

10. _____

How does each of the rituals you listed bring some consistency to your family life?

1. _____

2. _____

3. _____

4. _____

5. _____

6. _____

7. _____

8. _____

9. _____

10. _____

What are some rituals that you used to have in place but for one reason or another were stopped or interrupted?

1. _____

2. _____

3. _____

4. _____

5. _____

Which of the rituals you listed in the previous question would you consider starting up again?

1. _____

2. _____

3. _____

4. _____

5. _____

What difference might it make if you were to restart an old ritual?

_____

_____

_____

_____

_____

Schedule a meeting with your family. Invite them to talk about new rituals that you might implement in the future. Then list those rituals in the spaces provided.

1. _____

2. _____

3. _____

4. _____

5. _____

Take one of the new rituals that was decided upon by the family and try it a few times. Then write the results of that experiment in the spaces provided.

_____

_____

_____

_____

_____

Be sure to track those rituals that seem to provide consistency and stability and promote family cohesion.

55

Chores

THERAPIST'S OVERVIEW

Purpose of the Exercise

Household chores are often a source of conflict for families. In the past, chores were seen as a way of teaching children about responsibility. In modern households, with adults working more hours outside the home, children's chores are often seen as necessary to assure functioning of the household. Frequently, children are not as motivated as parents to do these everyday tasks. In addition, they may lack the organizational skills for success. This exercise is designed to encourage the entire family to see maintenance of the household as everyone's business. It then encourages everyone to participate in finding a solution. Many families find that when children are part of the decision-making process they are more invested in seeing that the plan works. This exercise also encourages parents to plan ahead rather than simply complain when things get out of hand.

Suggestions for Use

1. Suggest that maintenance of the household is everyone's concern.
2. Explore with family members the advantages of a smoother running household.
3. Encourage the family to revise the chores as frequently as necessary.
4. Once the family has had some success, explore what skills they used and ask how they might apply these skills to other situations.
5. After some success, explore the ways family members think and feel about each other.

EXERCISE

This exercise will help you with an issue that has plagued many families—chores. Because most households are very busy, participation from all family members is important. This exercise will help your children and adolescents in the decision-making process, and make sure that each person has his or her voice heard and that chores are evenly distributed. This can make the issue of chores a much easier one to manage.

To complete this exercise, start a list of all the chores that go into keeping a household together. Write down the list of chores in the spaces provided.

1. _____

2. _____

3. _____

4. _____

5. _____

6. _____

7. _____

8. _____

9. _____

10. _____

Next, look over the list. Are they all necessary or are there some that can be deleted or done less frequently? After determining this, in the spaces provided, write down the chores that are necessary and the frequency with which they need to be completed.

Daily Chores

1. _____

2. _____

3. _____

4. _____

5. _____

Weekly Chores

1. _____

2. _____

3. _____

4. _____

5. _____

Monthly Chores

1. _____

2. _____

3. _____

4. _____

5. _____

Next, hold a family meeting in which you all negotiate a fair division of labor. Keep in mind each person's age, available time, and ability. Then, create a plan for who will do what and when it will get done. Write the outcomes of this meeting in the spaces provided.

Person Responsible	**Chore**	**How Often Completed**
1. _____	_____	_____
2. _____	_____	_____
3. _____	_____	_____
4. _____	_____	_____
5. _____	_____	_____
6. _____	_____	_____
7. _____	_____	_____
8. _____	_____	_____
9. _____	_____	_____
10. _____	_____	_____

After completing the exercise, set a date to review your process and for fine-tuning.

Date: _____

Further consideration: If you think it is necessary, negotiate consequences for failure to fulfill obligations.

PART IV:
CHANGING ASPECTS OF CONTEXT

What's in a Problem?
Identifying Contextual Influences

THERAPIST'S OVERVIEW

Purpose of Exercise

Problems and solutions can be influenced by physiology, genetics, cognitive processes, culture, ethnicity, social factors, nutrition, gender, religion/spirituality, behavior, relationships, and so on. We refer to these as contextual propensities. Traditionally, mental health professionals' theories have dictated which of these components are more or less responsible for a problem and its resolution. However, psychotherapy outcome research has demonstrated that clients' theories are much more influential than therapists' theories in the solving of problems. Clients have ideas not only about how problems have developed and what has caused them but what it will take to solve them. Their theories are crucial in moving toward positive outcomes.

This exercise is designed to help parents, children, and adolescents identify those aspects of contexts that they think have influenced the problem and can be tapped into to solve it. By gaining a clear idea of clients' perspectives therapists can work with them to devise ways of helping them resolve their problems.

Suggestions for Use

1. This exercise may be used with parents and adolescents.
2. Challenge clients to determine the "makeup" of the problems they're facing. Do they think it's genetic and has been passed on from one generation to the other? Do they see the problem as being one that was learned?
3. Therapists can also help clients explore how various contextual influences might assist in solving their problem.
4. As a clinician, even though you may be cognitively oriented or a systems thinker, try to set your own beliefs aside in lieu of clients' beliefs and theories. Research has demonstrated that the closer that therapists match treatment with clients' beliefs about the cause of problems and what it will take to solve them, the chances of successful outcome increase.
5. This exercise can be combined with "Exploring Clients' Theories of Change."

EXERCISE

Because you have spent much time with the problem you've been facing, you know more about it than anyone else. Your expertise is important in determining what kinds of things have influenced the problem and what might help to solve it. For example, you may see the problem as being influenced by physiology, genetics, cognitive processes, culture, ethnicity, social factors, nutrition, gender, religion/spirituality, behavior, relationships, or some other propensity. This exercise will help you and your therapist learn more about what you see as influencing the problem you've been trying to solve.

To complete this exercise, first think about your experience with a specific problem that you've been facing. Then, for each question, check the corresponding space(s) or write down your response in the spaces provided.

Which of the following influences do you feel have contributed to the problem you're facing and/or may be helpful in solving it? (Check as many boxes as you feel are applicable)

Physiology/Biology	_____	Genetics	_____
Cognition/Thinking	_____	Culture/Ethnicity	_____
Social	_____	Nutrition	_____
Gender	_____	Religion/Spirituality	_____
General Relationships (friends, etc.)	_____	Family Relationships	_____
		Other	_____
Behavior	_____		

Transfer the influences that you checked into the spaces provided. Next, for each influence, place a "−" next to those influences that you feel have contributed to the problem and a "+" next to those that you feel may be helpful in solving it. For those influences that fit both categories use a "0." After you have assigned each influence a value, write down your explanation of how you think each particular influence has contributed to the problem, can assist with resolving the problem, or how it fits both categories.

Influence _____   Value _____

_____

_____

_____

_____

_____

Influence _____   Value _____

_____

_____

_____

_____

_____

Influence _____   Value _____

_____

_____

_____

_____

_____

Influence _____   Value _____

_____

_____

_____

_____

_____

Influence _____   Value _____

_____

_____

_____

_____

_____

Influence _____   Value _____

_____

_____

_____

_____

_____

Take a moment to review your responses. Where did the idea come from that these influences are contributing to the problem, can help with resolving the problem, or both? What is most important for your therapist to know about these influences?

_____

_____

_____

_____

_____

57

Tapping Resources:
Creating a Personal Inventory

THERAPIST'S OVERVIEW

Purpose of Exercise

This exercise follows "What's in a Problem? Identifying Contextual Influences." Once clients have identified the contextual influences that can be helpful in resolving their problems, it can be helpful to have them inventory the resources that they have to draw upon. These can then be utilized in efforts to solve the problem at hand.

The importance of client resources cannot be overstated. Psychotherapy outcome research has identified "extratherapeutic factors" as being the most significant contributor to outcome. A large portion of extratherapeutic factors relates to clients' strengths, abilities, and resources. Therapists who are making use of clients' resources are increasing the chance of positive outcome.

This exercise can help parents, children, and adolescents identify those resources that can be tapped into to assist in resolving the problem. These can include internal or external resources.

Suggestions for Use

1. This exercise can be completed individually, in pairs, as a family, with others who are involved, with or without a therapist, or in another arrangement that makes sense to the individual or family.
2. Challenge clients to identify and draw on resources from a multitude of areas in their lives.
3. Consider that what clients often see as deficits may in fact be strengths. For example, a parent who as a child was raised in extreme poverty may have learned the value of being economical.
4. This exercise will take some time. It's a good idea to talk with clients about how to approach it. For example, it can be done all at once, broken into smaller segments, etc.
5. Teens may have difficulty identifying their resources. Don't be discouraged if they are unable to do the exercise. Be slow to assume resistance. We believe that simply raising the possibility that they have resources will make it more likely that they will become aware of them.

Note: The exercise, "What's in a Problem? Identifying Contextual Influences," should be completed prior to beginning this exercise.

EXERCISE

In the exercise, "What's in a Problem? Identifying Contextual Influences," you identified those influences that you believe have contributed to the development of the problem and may be of help in resolving it. This exercise will assist you in creating an inventory of all your resources. These resources can be within you (internal) our in your environment (external). In the past, you may not have considered some of these to be resources.

To complete this exercise, study each of the areas listed, and consider what resources you may have that could be of assistance with the problem you're facing. Be as creative as possible. Then, in each area, write down your responses in the spaces provided.

Note: This exercise will take some time. There are many possibilities for completing it. For example, you may choose to do it all at once, break it into smaller parts, or approach it in some other way. You may also choose to talk with your therapist about how to approach it.

1. **Self**—This is about you. Ask yourself, "Who am I?" Then consider: What is it that makes you unique? What qualities do you possess? What aspects of yourself can you draw on in times of trouble? (If you already completed the exercise, "Who are You? Exploring the Qualities Within," you may want to refer back to it.)

How can who you are as a person be a resource for you?

_____

_____

_____

_____

_____

How can who you are as a person be of help with the problem you're facing?

_____

_____

_____

_____

_____

2. **Religion/Spirituality**—This includes, but is not limited to: attending church, praying, meditation, singing, chanting, belief in a higher power, remembering that each person is a child of God, imagining your connection to universal love, having a sense that Jesus, Mohammed, Allah, Zoroaster, or Buddha is with you, and so on. If you do not practice an organized religion, think about your personal understanding of your place in the universe and how that affects your everyday decisions.

How is religion/spirituality a resource for you?

_____

_____

_____

_____

How can religion/spirituality help you with the problem you're facing?

_____

_____

_____

_____

3. **Culture and/or Ethnicity**—*Culture* is a sort of "mental blueprint" of patterns including shared thoughts, symbols, beliefs, values, customs, behaviors, and artifacts that you and your family members use to cope with the world and with one another, and that were learned in society and transmitted from generation to generation. *Ethnicity* is a culture within a culture. In other words, you and your family may be part of a smaller group of people with a common or shared identity, living within a larger, mainstream group. Although you are part of it, you may have some ways of thinking and doing things that differ from the mainstream group.

How is your cultural and/or ethnic background a resource for you?

_____

_____

_____

_____

How can your cultural and/or ethnic background help you with the problem you're facing?

_____

_____

_____

_____

4. **Gender**—Consider: What is it like for you to be a man or woman in this world? Raising children? What does being a man or woman allow you to do? (It is acknowledged that gender inequalities exist and oppress people, women in particular. What is important here is to view gender as a resource. For example, perhaps being a female who grew up in a family with five males helped you to better understand and deal with the behavior of males.)

How is your gender a resource for you?

_____

_____

_____

_____

How can your gender help you with the problem you're facing?

_____

_____

_____

_____

5. **Relationships**—This includes, but is not limited to: family, friends, co-workers, colleagues, teachers, religious or spiritual guides, scout leaders, coaches, and so on.

How are your relationships a resource for you?

_____

_____

_____

_____

How can your relationships help you with the problem you're facing?

_____

_____

_____

_____

6. **Employment/School**—This includes, but is not limited to: being employed in a specific type of job, working at a specific company, business, or agency, practicing or learning a trade, taking classes, and so on.

How is your employment/school a resource for you?

_____

_____

_____

_____

How can your employment/school help you with the problem you're facing?

_____

_____

_____

7. **Community**—Consider the quote, "It takes a village to raise a child." What does that mean to you? Community can include any resource at a local, county, state, or federal level. It can also include, but is not limited to: cultural surroundings, social networks, clubs, associations, boards, and so on.

How is your community a resource for you?

_____

_____

_____

_____

How can your community help you with the problem you're facing?

_____

_____

_____

_____

Now that you have compiled an extensive list of resources, take some time to make sure that you have included everything that you can think of. Include others' perspectives if necessary. Then, consider how you can begin to utilize your resources to solve the current problem you're facing and perhaps future ones as well. You may also want to consult with your therapist about your inventory.

58

How Am I Supposed to Be?
Challenging Unhelpful Influences

THERAPIST'S OVERVIEW

Purpose of Exercise

Actor Christopher Reeve once said, "I'm more than just my body." The parents, children, and adolescents with whom we work are bigger than any one aspect of themselves. There are cultural, ethnic, societal, biological and genetic, relational (family, friends, work, etc.), religious and spiritual, and other contextual influences, which, to varying degrees, extend beyond the physical person. For some clients, being able to draw on religious or cultural upbringing and beliefs, for example, can be enough to get them through times of trouble. Conversely, there are times when contextual influences can keep them from moving on. The task of the clinician is in honoring clients' beliefs and all aspects of who they are while simultaneously searching for possibilities for change.

This exercise is designed to help parents, children, and adolescents identify ways in which contextual influences sometimes restrict their views and close down possibilities for change. It can also help therapists to work with clients in a way that is respectful of clients' beliefs and practices yet allows clients to subtly challenge their own personal views and find possibilities for change.

Suggestions for Use

1. This exercise may be used with parents and adolescents.
2. It is very important that therapists do not imply in any way that the ways clients view the world is "wrong" or "bad." Instead, they should acknowledge, validate, and show respect for their beliefs. The key is to work with clients so that they challenge their own beliefs and open up possibilities for future change.
3. This exercise relies on therapists learning from clients what has worked or might work for them. When allowed to take on the role, clients are our best teachers.

Note: This exercise is to be paired with, "What's in a Problem? Identifying Contextual Influences." It can also be helpful, but is not required, to complete "Tapping Resources: Creating a Personal Inventory" prior to this exercise.

EXERCISE

Each one of us is influenced by culture, ethnicity, society, biology and genetics, relationships (family, friends, work, etc.), religion and spirituality, and other contextual influences to varying degrees. We are more than just a body. We can draw on these influences to get us through tough times. For example, a belief in a higher power can give us some strength to move on. At other times, such influences can contribute to the problem we're experiencing and be a factor in becoming stuck.

This exercise will help you to take a look at the contextual influences in your life and to consider how they may be restricting you in solving your problem. This exercise is not to pass judgment on your beliefs. Your beliefs are valid. Instead, it is designed to help you consider how you can retain your beliefs and work within them to find possibilities for solving the problem that you're facing with your son or daughter.

If you haven't already done so, please complete the exercise, "What's in a Problem? Identifying Contextual Influences," before beginning this one. It will help you get a better idea of the influences in your life.

To complete this exercise, first refer back to your answers for the exercise, "What's in a Problem? Identifying Contextual Influences." Find the influences that you assigned a value of "–" or "0." Next, write those influences in the spaces provided.

Influence _____   Value _____

_____

_____

_____

Influence _____   Value _____

_____

_____

_____

Influence _____   Value _____

_____

_____

_____

Influence _____   Value _____

_____

_____

_____

Influence _____   Value _____

_____

_____

_____

For the next part of this exercise, with each influence, ask yourself a few or all of the following questions. (If necessary use another piece of paper to write down your answers):

1. How does this particular influence restrict me in trying to solve the problem?
2. How can I continue to hold onto my beliefs and solve the problem at the same time?
3. What are other possible interpretations of the problem I'm dealing with that are consistent with my beliefs?
4. What would my beliefs allow me to do to solve the problem I'm facing that I haven't already considered or tried?
5. Who do I know that has faced the same problem and has solved it? Would the way they solved it be consistent with my beliefs?
6. Who do I know that holds the same beliefs that I do that might be able to help me with this problem? If I don't know, how can I find out?
7. What might other people in other parts of the world who have the same beliefs do to solve this problem? If I don't know, how can I find out?

When you're done, take a few moments to reflect on your responses. What did you learn? How might you approach your problem differently than before but in a way that is consistent with your values and beliefs?

_____

_____

_____

_____

_____

Hang on to this paper and review it when you're trying to resolve a problem that is being influenced by some aspect of context. Also consider bringing it to your next therapy session and talking it over with your therapist.

59

Those Who Know Me Best

THERAPIST'S OVERVIEW

Purpose of Exercise

All human beings face difficulty from time to time. One of the ways that we are able to move through our pain and suffering is through the help of others. In fact, if you ask most people, they will identify at least one person who made a difference in their lives at one point or another. By identifying such persons, we can reorient clients to times when they felt acknowledged and understood, when they accessed past resources, and tapped into previous solutions to problems.

This exercise is designed to help parents, children, and adolescents to identify present and past relationships that helped them through difficult times. Once these relationships have been identified, we can help clients to determine how those relationships were helpful to them. This can help clients negotiate their difficulties and get back on track.

Suggestions for Use

1. This exercise may be used with parents and adolescents.
2. Even though we are asking clients to recall past relationships, it's not necessary for the person who helped out to be available in the present. What we want to know is how the relationship helped the client. For example, if a client said, "I really wish my dad were around, he understood me." Although we cannot bring back a deceased parent we can ask, "What was it about your relationship with your father that helped you through times of trouble?" We then find out that the client felt heard and understood. We can then follow with, "So when you feel heard and understood that helps you through times of trouble."
3. Some clients will think of many persons that helped them out while others will struggle to identify just one. Therefore, it can sometimes be helpful to go through different scenes of their lives and ask them to identify significant people during those times. We can then ask, "Tell me about the role that _____ played in your life at that time."

EXERCISE

What do movies such as *Mr. Holland's Opus, The Karate Kid, Dangerous Minds,* and *October Sky* have in common? They all portray the significance that family members, friends, teachers, coaches, scout leaders, and others can have. Growing up, most people can identify a person or several people who were there for them in times of trouble, helped them to solve problems, get through difficult times, and for some, helped them to stay alive.

This exercise will help you identify those people who have made a difference in your life in the past. Keep in mind that it's not always necessary for those people to still be around. Oftentimes, just reminding ourselves of what we gained from our relationships with such persons is enough to get us back on track. In addition, notice that there are questions for adolescents and adults and additional ones for those who are also parents.

To complete this exercise, write down your responses in the spaces provided.

For Adolescents and Adults

Whom have you met in your life who would understand exactly what you've been going through?

_____

_____

How is that helpful for you to know?

_____

_____

If you could speak with that person, what would he or she suggest that you do?

_____

_____

When things were going better for you, who was around to help you out and make a difference in your life?

_____

_____

What did that person say or do?

_____

_____

Whom do you look up to? How come?

_____

_____

When you're struggling, who knows exactly what to say/do to help you get back on track?

_____

_____

What might that person suggest that you do now to get back on track?

_____

_____

What would it take for you to follow that suggestion a little bit now?

_____

_____

For Parents

When you're questioning yourself as a parent, who accepts you unconditionally, understands what you're going through, and would never blame you?

_____

_____

How would that person help you?

_____

_____

What do you need from others when you're struggling as a parent?

_____

_____

(Other than yourself) Who in your child's or adolescent's life seems to be able to get through to him or her? How does that person(s) do that?

_____

_____

What have you noticed about how that person gets through to your son or daughter?

_____

_____

Whom do you know that your son or daughter is close to who might be willing to help out with the problem you're experiencing?

_____

_____

Most of the time, there are others who have helped us out in the past and would do so again in the present and future if we asked for their help. More important, reminding ourselves of what we need and how we were able to attain those things in the past, in times of trouble, can help us to get back on track.

60

Have You Ever . . . ?

THERAPIST'S OVERVIEW

Purpose of Exercise

An upside of experiencing problems with children and adolescents is that others have often had similar experiences and some will have met with success. Employing the help of such experienced persons can sometimes free parents to think about things differently. Just having multiple perspectives to choose from can present parents with a smorgasbord of ideas. In addition, children and adolescents frequently have friends or acquaintances that have already gone through what they're currently going through and may have ideas that can be helpful.

The purpose of this exercise is to help parents, children, and adolescents to expand their views of their situations by utilizing support systems and external resources. This can help them to gain new perspectives on the problems they're facing and perhaps approach solving them in new ways.

Suggestions for Use

1. This exercise can be used with parents and adolescents.
2. It's important to remind parents and adolescents that even though others may have ideas about how they should approach their problems, ideas are just ideas. Just because something has worked for one person or family does not mean that it will work for someone else. Clients should feel free to accept and act on only those ideas that fit with them.
3. If parents or adolescents don't have access to others, have them speculate about what those persons might suggest.

EXERCISE

When experiencing problems, it's important to remember that we're not alone. Many times others have had similar experiences and may have even had success in dealing with those problems. As a parent or adolescent, you may also have friends or acquaintances that have gone through in the past what you're currently going through. In both cases, those in our social support systems sometimes have ideas that can help us solve our problems.

This exercise will help you connect with others and elicit their ideas about how to deal with the problems you're experiencing. Keep in mind that others' ideas are just ideas. Just because something worked for someone else doesn't mean that it's right for you or that it will work for you. Therefore, you will need to use your discretion when asking others for their ideas.

To complete this exercise, place your responses to the questions in the spaces provided.

List the names of five or more people whose opinions and ideas you value and respect. These can be people who have experienced the same problem you are experiencing or those whose opinions you simply value and respect.

1. _____

2. _____

3. _____

4. _____

5. _____

Approach at least three of these people and explain your situation to them. Then ask them for their ideas about how to approach your problem. Pay close attention to any skills that they mention they use or have used to solve similar problems. Write their names and responses in the spaces provided.

1. Name   Response

_____   _____

_____

2. Name   Response

_____   _____

_____

3. Name   Response

_____   _____

_____

What surprised you most about their responses?

_____

_____

_____

_____

_____

Which ideas did you find most useful? Why?

Idea

_____

_____

_____

Idea

_____

_____

_____

Idea

_____

_____

_____

How will this influence what you do in regard to the problem you're facing?

_____

_____

_____

_____

When stuck with a problem, consider using this exercise to expand your own perspective on how to approach solving it. Also consider talking with your therapist about what you found out.

61

Exploring Family Solutions

THERAPIST'S OVERVIEW

Purpose of Exercise

For many parents, children, and adolescents in crisis, their families of origin can be an excellent resource. Families can offer emotional support including assistance with child care, shoulders to lean on, guidance, and a wealth of experiences that have brought about solutions. This exercise is designed to help parents, children, and adolescents who are experiencing problems to use their families of origin as a resource for finding solutions.

Suggestions for Use

1. This exercise can be used individually with parents, children, and adolescents, or as a family project. Remember that family is not limited to biological ties, it can also include anyone who has had any involvement in the client's life.
2. This exercise can be difficult for some family members who view their families of origin in a primarily negative way and would not ordinarily ask for their assistance. In such cases, it can be helpful to suggest to them, "Many times members of our families have had experience in dealing with the problems that we are now faced with. We don't have to do the same thing that they did to solve their problems, but it can be helpful to at least learn what they did to achieve success. We can then decide for ourselves what's right for us."
3. In the event that a parent or other hesitates, this exercise can also be done without actually contacting other family members. This simply requires the person to rely more on memory and to speculate more about other family members.

EXERCISE

We've all learned how to do things from a variety of different sources. We're in a constant state of learning. A main resource for many of us is our family of origin. Families can provide emotional support and guidance in times of trouble. In addition, family members have often gone through and had success with some of the things that we are currently having trouble with. This exercise will help you to consider your family as a possible resource for problems. It can be completed in one of two ways: (1) By approaching family members (2) By using our memories or speculating about family members.

To complete this exercise, write your responses in the spaces provided.

1. Who in your family are you close to? Please list each member.

    1. _____

    2. _____

    3. _____

    4. _____

    5. _____

2. What do you appreciate most about them? Please list something about each family member.

    1. _____

    2. _____

    3. _____

    4. _____

    5. _____

3. If you needed their help, how might they provide that help? Please list something about each family member.

    1. _____

    2. _____

    3. _____

    4. _____

    5. _____

4. Which of the family members you previously listed would you feel most comfortable approaching about the problem you're experiencing?

    1. _____

    2. _____

    3. _____

    4. _____

    5. _____

5. Select one or two family members that you would feel comfortable in approaching and tell them about your situation. Be sure to inform them about the kind of assistance you are seeking so they know how to help you. After doing this, list their responses. (If you prefer to not approach any family members skip to question #8.)

1. _____

2. _____

3. _____

4. _____

5. _____

6. Which responses fit best with you and your situation? Why?

1. _____

2. _____

3. _____

4. _____

5. _____

7. What might you do with this information from family members?

_____

_____

_____

_____

8. Who in your family has successfully dealt (to any degree) with the problem or one similar to the one you're experiencing? How did they do that? How is it helpful to you to know about their experience with the same or a similar problem?

_____

_____

_____

_____

9. What qualities do your family members possess that they were able to stand up to such adversity?

_____

_____

_____

_____

10. What does that tell you about your family?

_____

_____

_____

_____

Be sure to review this sheet or complete a new one when you're facing a problem that you believe your family might be able to help with. Also consider discussing it with your therapist.

62

Is It Inherited or Learned or . . . ?

THERAPIST'S OVERVIEW

Purpose of Exercise

A common theory amongst families who are experiencing behavioral problems with their children or adolescents is the idea that the problems are inherited and passed along from generation to generation. In addition, when looking at their family histories, it's also common for parents and others to say things such as, "He got his hyperactivity from his father," "Her mother is the same way—she's very emotional," or "Alcoholism runs in our family." When referring to their families of origin many will focus on negative predispositions, traits that were inherited, or behaviors that were learned. In a similar way, therapists have traditionally been educated as pathology seekers. They've been trained to discover "what's wrong" within families.

This exercise is designed to help parents, children, and adolescents move beyond the idea that what is inherited from family members is primarily negative. Through the use of the question, "What's right?" therapists can help parents, children, and adolescents to explore strengths and abilities that they may have inherited or learned from their families of origin.

Suggestions for Use

1. This exercise may be used with parents and adolescents.
2. This exercise can be difficult for some family members who view their families of origin in a primarily negative way. In such cases it can be helpful to suggest to them, "Many times we see things in ourselves that we don't like and believe that those things came from our families. However, in all of us are wonderful qualities; some of which we inherited or learned from our parents and other family members. What are the good qualities that you think you may have inherited or behaviors that you may have learned from your family?"
3. Qualities can be anything from being a good listener, to liking business-oriented work, to being a quick learner, to liking animals. There are endless possibilities. The same holds true for behaviors.

EXERCISE

As human beings we are made up of many influences. One of these influences is our genes and what we've inherited from our families of origin. Another is what we have learned from other family members. Yet we don't always look at what we've inherited or learned from our families in a positive light. This exercise will help you to explore those strengths and abilities that you, your children, and other family members may have inherited or learned. These traits, qualities, and behaviors can be resources for you in solving difficulties in the present.

To complete this exercise, write your responses in the spaces provided.

What do you feel are your best qualities?

1. _____

2. _____

3. _____

4. _____

5. _____

6. _____

7. _____

8. _____

9. _____

10. _____

Place a check mark next to the qualities that you think may have been, at least in part, inherited or learned from your family of origin.

What do you do well?

1. _____

2. _____

3. _____

4. _____

5. _____

6. _____

7. _____

8. _____

9. _____

10. _____

Place a check mark next to the qualities that you think may have been, at least in part, inherited or learned from your family of origin.

Who else in your family shares some of the same qualities and/or abilities that you have?

1. _____

2. _____

3. _____

4. _____

5. _____

What do those qualities allow you to do that you might not otherwise be able to do had you not been born in or raised by your family?

_____

_____

_____

_____

_____

Take time to review your responses. Consider revising this sheet as you learn more about yourself and your family of origin.

63

Who Am I Like?
Speculating About My Parents

THERAPIST'S OVERVIEW

Purpose of Exercise

Unfortunately, there are many children, adolescents, and adults who know little or nothing about their families of origin. Furthermore, sometimes what they do know isn't pleasant. In most cases, whether information is available or not, these persons are speculating about what their parents were really like. Many wonder if they are anything like their biological parents. This exercise will help children, adolescents, and adults draw on their own qualities and abilities as they speculate about their biological parents. This can help them to build inner strength to face current and future problems.

Suggestions for Use

1. This exercise is for parents, children, and adolescents.
2. This exercise can be especially useful for children and adolescents in residential placements, group homes, and foster homes. It can also be helpful for those who have been adopted and will likely never learn more about their biological parents.
3. With or without information, some clients will already have created ideas about their biological parents. These views can be very negative. In such cases it can be helpful to say, "There are things that you know about your parents that you don't like. But I'm also curious because you are very _____ (fill in the blank—kind, outgoing, mechanical, etc.) and I wonder if you inherited any of that from your parents. I suspect that there are some things about your mother/father/parents that were wonderful and don't quite fit with the picture you have of her/him/them."

EXERCISE

From time to time some of us wonder if we're more like our mother, father, or a combination of both. But not all of us know much about our parents. For a variety of reasons, we may have little or no information about one or both of them. But this doesn't stop us from speculating about what they were like. On the other hand, if we do know a lot about them, sometimes we only focus on the parts of them that we don't like or that we don't want to be like. When we do this we can leave out other wonderful parts of them. This exercise can help you to speculate about your biological parents and simultaneously learn more about yourself in the process.

To complete this exercise, write your responses in the spaces provided.

1. Based on your own thoughts and what you have learned about them, what do you think your biological mother or father might have been like?

_____

_____

_____

_____

_____

2. What, if anything, does that say about the kind of person you are?

_____

_____

_____

_____

_____

3. If you have a negative view of your biological parents, where did that view come from? (If you do not have a negative view of your biological parents, skip to question #7).

_____

_____

_____

_____

_____

4. When have you thought to yourself that maybe there were parts of the story about your parents that were inaccurate or left out? What do you think might have been inaccurate or left out?

_____

_____

_____

_____

_____

5. If you were to accept that maybe you and/or others didn't have all of the story or the facts right how might your ideas about your mother and/or father change? And, what difference would that make for you?

_____

_____

_____

_____

_____

6. In your mind, what are your best qualities?

   1. _____

   2. _____

   3. _____

   4. _____

   5. _____

7. What would others say are your best qualities?

   1. _____

   2. _____

   3. _____

   4. _____

   5. _____

8. What do you think you do well?

   1. _____

   2. _____

   3. _____

   4. _____

   5. _____

9. What would others say you do well?

1. _____

2. _____

3. _____

4. _____

5. _____

10. Based on the type of person you are, your personal qualities, and what you do well, what ideas do you have about what your mother or father might have been like?

_____

_____

_____

_____

_____

11. Genetically speaking, we all, at least to some degree, inherit different things from our biological parents. What percentage of who you are as a person, including your inner qualities and abilities, do you think is inherited?

_____ %

As you look at this percentage, what do you speculate about regarding your mother and/or father?

_____

_____

_____

_____

_____

12. What new ideas do you have as a result of that speculation?

_____

_____

_____

_____

_____

13. How can those new ideas be helpful to you in solving current or future problems?

_____

_____

_____

_____

14. If you knew that you could pass along certain qualities and skills that you inherited to future generations, which ones would you choose?

1. _____

2. _____

3. _____

4. _____

5. _____

15. What does that say about the kind of person you are?

_____

_____

_____

_____

As you reflect on your responses, remember that there are many influences that contribute to who we are as people. Although there may be things that we would rather erase or forget about regarding our biological parents and our pasts, there are also things that were passed on to us that make us good people and encourage us to speak differently about our parents.

Refer back to this as needed and consider discussing it with your therapist.

– 64 –

Reviving Your Soul:
Tapping Spiritual Energy and Resources

THERAPIST'S OVERVIEW

Purpose of Exercise

We draw on different resources to revitalize ourselves, create meaning in our lives, and to solve problems. One area in particular that can be an excellent resource is spirituality. By tapping into spiritual resources, parents can increase their energy and perhaps gain a new perspective on approaching and finding solutions for the problems they're facing. This can also be useful to adolescents who are seeking direction and meaning in life.

The purpose of this exercise is to help parents tap into spirituality and utilize it as a resource for increasing their energy, gaining new perspectives, and for solving problems with their children and adolescents.

Suggestions for Use

1. This exercise is primarily for use with parents and adolescents. However, it can be modified for use with younger children by changing the language of the questions.
2. Spirituality is a personal consideration. It is important that we allow clients to draw on it in a way that makes the most sense for them.

EXERCISE

For many people, a consistent resource in their lives is spirituality. Whether it's attending church, praying, meditating, chanting, reading scripture, or through other means, having a connection to spirituality can provide support, comfort, renewed energy, direction, and even help with problem solving. This exercise is designed to help you tap into spirituality to increase your energy and perhaps gain a new perspective on finding solutions for the problems you are facing with your son or daughter. This can also be a helpful exercise for your adolescent if he or she is the type of person seeking meaning or direction.

We will approach spirituality in three ways in this exercise. To complete this exercise, take a moment to review each method for finding your spiritual pathway. Then consider the questions that follow and write your responses in the spaces provided.

1. *Remember past spiritual experiences and connection.* One of the most effective ways for solving problems is to recall previous times when things went well or when you solved problems, and reuse those skills.

Have you ever had religious or spiritual beliefs or followed religious or spiritual practices? If so, how have they been helpful to you in any way?

_____

_____

_____

_____

Have you ever felt connected to something more than yourself, such as nature, humanity, the universe, or God? If so, how has that been a resource for you?

_____

_____

_____

_____

What, if anything, has been your most profound spiritual experience? What did you learn from it?

_____

_____

_____

_____

2. *Recognize present spiritual resources and solutions.* Search in your present life for ways to access spirituality.

What do you do or where do you go to recharge yourself when you get a chance? How does that help you?

_____

_____

_____

_____

How do you connect with other people?

_____

_____

_____

_____

Do you think you have a purpose for being alive? If so, what is it? What does that purpose do for you?

_____

_____

_____

_____

A bumper sticker seen on a BMW said, "The one who dies with the most toys wins." What is your yardstick for measuring success in life?

_____

_____

_____

_____

Are you aware of any spiritual figure or activity that you think might help you develop your spirituality? If so, how might that figure or activity be a resource for you?

_____

_____

_____

_____

3. *Create future spiritual hopes and intentions.* If it's been difficult for you to access spirituality in the past or present, it can be helpful to look to the future to create some new possibilities in the present.

What kind of spiritual or religious activities would you like to do in the future, if any? How might that help you?

_____

_____

_____

_____

Is there any area of your spiritual life that you would like to develop more? If so, what is it?

_____

_____

_____

_____

Is there any spiritual or religious figure that you would like to use as a model for you, your adolescent, or your family? In what way?

_____

_____

_____

_____

If spirituality were to become more of a resource for you in the future, what difference might that make in your life? What difference would it make with the problem you face?

_____

_____

_____

_____

Keep this sheet nearby as a reminder of how spirituality might be a resource for you.

65

Who's Driving the Bus?
Promoting Accountability

THERAPIST'S OVERVIEW

Purpose of Exercise

Many children and adolescents take and benefit from psychotropic medications. For others, a psychiatric diagnosis can be helpful in explaining behavior, removing blame, and in accessing services. At the same time, there is a risk in utilizing any external agent. In the eyes of parents, children, and adolescents the external agent (e.g., medication, psychiatric diagnosis, etc.) can become the factor in determining behavior and action. For example, they may view the medication or diagnosis as being in charge. The problem with this is that some people will deny accountability and say things such as, "I couldn't help it, my mom forgot to give me my medication" or "He has ADD and he does that because he's impulsive." Although medication can help people *feel* better, ultimately, it is up to the individual to make choices and be accountable for his or her behavior.

The purpose of this exercise is to help parents promote accountability with their children and adolescents when external agents are involved. In addition, therapists can learn to identify statements of nonaccountability and make small changes in language to promote accountability.

Suggestions for Use

1. This exercise is mainly for parents who have children and/or adolescents who are taking psychotropic medication, have a psychiatric diagnosis, or in cases where there is some external agent involved that is affecting change. However, it can be used in a general way to promote accountability of any kind.
2. This exercise is especially for teaching parents about nonaccountability but can be modified to use with children and adolescents.
3. It's important when psychotropic medications are involved that therapists, parents, children, and adolescents understand what those medications are *supposed* to do. It is very common for clients to have a misunderstanding of how a particular medication is supposed to work, which can dramatically effect how they approach problem behavior. In addition, parents should be educated on specific psychiatric diagnoses when they are assigned to their children or adolescents.
4. This can be an excellent role-play exercise for those working on enhancing their listening skills.

EXERCISE

Many children and adolescents benefit from psychotropic medications. A psychiatric diagnosis can provide answers and relief. At the same time, there is a risk whenever external agents such as medication and diagnosis are introduced. If you've ever heard your son or daughter say something like, "I couldn't help it, I didn't get my medication this morning" or "I've got ADHD so I can't sit still," then you've heard a statement of nonaccountability. That is, your son or daughter was implying that he or she did not have a choice in how to behave and that something else was in charge of his or her behavior. This is a dangerous idea. Certainly psychotropic medications can help children and adolescents *feel* better, but these medications do not make decisions for them nor do they control behavior or actions.

This exercise is designed to help you to identify when your son or daughter is avoiding being accountable—denying responsibility for his or her behavior. In turn, you will learn how to promote accountability by making small changes in language and in how you respond to your son or daughter.

There are three ways of promoting accountability when children and adolescents are making statements implying that they have no choice and are not accountable for their actions and behaviors. To complete this exercise, review each method for promoting accountability. Then, following the examples, write your responses to the statements in the spaces provided.

1. Reflect back nonaccountability statements without the nonaccountability part. When you hear your son or daughter use an excuse or explanation that conveys nonaccountability repeat those statements while dropping the nonaccountability part.

Examples

CHILD: He called me a name so I hit him.
PARENT: You hit him.

ADOLESCENT: You forgot to give me my medication so I couldn't remember to come home on time.
PARENT: You didn't come home on time.

Child: I have ADD so I couldn't do my homework.
Parent: _____

Adolescent: What did you expect? You didn't remind me so I didn't get up for school.
Parent: _____

Statement by your son/daughter: _____

_____

Your response: _____

_____

2. *Find counterexamples that indicate choice or accountability.* Search for examples in which your son or daughter behaved or acted in a way that demonstrated accountability, thereby contradicting his or her claims of nonaccountability.

Examples

CHILD: I can't help it. If I don't get my medicine, I can't control my anger.
PARENT: I'm confused, last Thursday you didn't get your medicine and you did a great job of controlling your anger. How did you do that?

ADOLESCENT: I'll never get my homework done anyway, so why should I even try?
PARENT: I must be missing something. How did you manage to get your homework done earlier in the semester?

Child: If she makes me mad, she's gonna get what she deserves—a fat lip.
Parent: _____

Adolescent: I can't help it, you didn't remind me to bring my books.
Parent: _____

Statement by your son/daughter: _____

_____

Your response: _____

_____

3. *Use the word "and" to link together feelings and accountability.* Give your son or daughter permission to feel whatever he or she feels while simultaneously holding him or her accountable for his or her behaviors and actions.

Examples

CHILD: He makes me mad so I hit him.
PARENT: It's okay to be mad and it's not okay to hit him.

ADOLESCENT: I'm so pissed off! You need to let me come home at midnight!
PARENT: You can be pissed off and you need to be in at eleven-thirty.

Child: If she would keep her mouth shut and not make me mad I wouldn't go off on her.
Parent: _____

Adolescent: Drinking helps me not feel sad.
Parent: _____

Statement by your son/daughter: _____

_____

Your response: _____

_____

Take time to practice picking up on language that makes excuses or explanations and conveys nonaccountability. Then use the methods you've learned to help your child or adolescent take responsibility for his or her behaviors and actions.

PART V:
KEEPING THE BALL ROLLING

66

Keeping an Eye on Change Between Sessions

THERAPIST'S OVERVIEW

Purpose of Exercise

Between therapy sessions, it can be helpful to orient clients toward change. This is supported by outcome research, which suggests that therapy should be change-focused. That is, emphasis should be on how things change as opposed to how people remain stuck in their problems. The fact is, although change is constant, clients often become oriented toward what isn't working and they remain stuck. In actuality, most problems either get better or worse between sessions—they don't remain the same.

The purpose of this exercise is to help parents focus more on change by orienting them toward what's working in their lives and identifying possible solutions. This can help to identify "what's right" in their lives.

Suggestions for Use

1. This exercise can be used in a session individually with any family member or with the entire family. It can also be used as an exercise between sessions.
2. This exercise can be used for people in or out of therapy. If the person(s) using this exercise is not in therapy, he or she can focus on what changes from week to week, for example, as opposed from session to session.
3. If you have used this exercise, it is important that when clients return for second and subsequent sessions that you acknowledge and validate their feelings and points of view before delving into what's working or what has changed. If this is not done, a percentage of clients will feel unheard and unacknowledged and will tune us out or appear resistant when we ask for the results of the exercise.
4. It can be helpful to familiarize clients with action-talk by having them do the exercise, "The Language of Change: Using Action-Talk" before completing this exercise.

EXERCISE

Things are always changing. This includes the problems that we face. Even though it can seem as if problems stay the same, aspects such as intensity or frequency are always in flux. Sometimes they're more manageable than others. Yet when we're dealing with problems, especially those involving children and adolescents, we don't always notice when things are going better. If we do, we find ourselves waiting for the other shoe to drop, thinking, "This will never last." This exercise will help you shift your attention to "what's right" and what's working with your situation by helping you notice what's happening between your therapy sessions. By orienting your attention in this way you may be able to see some new ways of approaching the problem with your son or daughter.

To complete this exercise, follow the directions and write your responses in the spaces provided. Between now and the next therapy session, notice the things that your son or daughter is doing and what is happening in your relationship with him or her that you would like to have continue.

What did you notice your son or daughter doing or happening in your relationship with him or her that you would like to have continue? Be as specific as possible, listing each behavior, action, or interaction by using clear, action-based descriptions.

1. _____

2. _____

3. _____

4. _____

5. _____

6. _____

7. _____

8. _____

9. _____

10. _____

What was it that allowed more favorable actions by your son or daughter and/or interactions between you and him or her to occur?

_____

_____

_____

_____

_____

What difference did it make for you that those behaviors happened with your son or daughter and/or that you and he or she got along differently?

_____

_____

_____

_____

_____

What will it take to keep those desirable behaviors and interactions going?

_____

_____

_____

_____

_____

As you look back on the time between sessions (or over the past week), what did you learn about yourself? Your son or daughter?

_____

_____

_____

_____

_____

Bring this sheet to your next session and discuss it with your therapist, or talk about it with your son or daughter and/or family.

67

Where's the Evidence?

THERAPIST'S OVERVIEW

Purpose of the Exercise

When facing problems, it makes sense to most people to become problem-focused. Although this can tell one a lot about the problem itself, it also keeps the focus on what's going wrong. It also keeps attention on what parents don't want as opposed to what they do want. This is a creative exercise that can help parents, children, and adolescents to shift their attention away from studying problems to searching for evidence that things are changing and heading in a better direction.

The purpose of this exercise is to help children and younger adolescents to collect "evidence" that they are changing and for parents to also take note of those changes. This can help clients to become change-focused as opposed to problem-focused.

Suggestions for Use

1. This exercise will be most applicable to children and younger adolescents. Older adolescents may not be as interested in the process involved.
2. This can be presented as a "mission" or "challenge" to children to prove who they *really* are.
3. The handouts offered in this exercise can be duplicated as frequently as needed.

EXERCISE

This exercise will help your child or young adolescent collect evidence that he or she is changing his or her behavior and beginning to head in a preferred direction. It will also help you focus on the behavior that you want with your child as opposed to what you do not want.

To do this, you will use "Letters of Evidence" and an "Evidence Log." Letters of Evidence represent specific instances of change that are noticeable by others. Parents, teachers, juvenile officers, coaches, scout leaders, and so on who have noticed positive change with the child can fill out and sign these letters. These letters can include, but are not limited to, good grades, good behavior, positive actions, helping others, and volunteering, etc. Evidence does not have to be in the form of the letter. It can simply be a paper with an improved grade, a report card, a merit badge, or some other evidence. Evidence Logs are the form that the evidence gets logged on. This way, the evidence that is being collected can be tracked. It's often a good idea to put an Evidence Log where it is readily visible to remind your son or daughter of his or her changes and accomplishments.

To complete this exercise, make a copy of each of the forms on the following two pages, and begin to put them into action.

OFFICIAL
LETTER OF EVIDENCE

Name: _____

Week of: _____

Type of Evidence:

_____

_____ ___

_____

_____

_____

_____

_____

_____

_____

_____

_____

_____

Verified by: _____

Date: _____

MY EVIDENCE LOG

Name: _____

Week of: _____

☺ 1.

☺ 2.

☺ 3.

☺ 4.

☺ 5.

☺ 6.

☺ 7.

68

Identifying and Amplifying Change

THERAPIST'S OVERVIEW

Purpose of Exercise

Because change can happen at any time, we are on a constant lookout for what is different with clients and the problems they're facing. To do this we focus on *identifying* and *amplifying* change. In identifying change, clients notice what has been better. Amplifying change relates to how the change came about. We can find out about these things either by asking clients questions in our sessions or by having them do an exercise that helps them identify and amplify change.

The purpose of this exercise is to help clients identify and amplify changes that they have made in relation to their problems. In addition, therapists are offered questions that they can ask clients to help them identify what has changed and how that change came about.

Suggestions for Use

1. This exercise can be used individually with any family member or as a group exercise for the entire family.
2. This exercise can be used by people in or out of therapy. If the person(s) using this exercise is not in therapy, he or she can focus on what changes from week to week, as opposed to session to session.
3. If you have used this exercise, it is important that when clients return for second and subsequent sessions that you acknowledge and validate their feelings and points of view before delving into what has changed. If this is not done, some clients will feel unheard and unacknowledged and will tune us out or appear resistant when we ask for the results of the exercise.
4. It can be helpful to familiarize clients with action-talk by having them do the exercise, "The Language of Change: Using Action-Talk" before completing this exercise.
5. Even though positive change may have happened, because clients are experiencing other problems or have other things on their minds, they often don't immediately notice the change. Therefore, it's important to remain change-focused and patient. Look for small changes rather than all-or-nothing change.

EXERCISE

Even though change is happening all the time, we don't always notice it. It can become especially difficult to notice positive change when life seems to present one dilemma after another.

Yet if we take the time to notice what and how things are changing in relation to the problems we are facing, we often notice that much is different. This exercise will help you to identify positive changes that have occurred with the problem you've been facing with your son or daughter and how that change came about. You can then work to build upon these changes until the problem is more manageable or it is no longer a problem.

To complete this exercise, write your responses to the questions in the spaces provided.

What have you noticed that has changed for the better with the problem you've been facing? Be as specific as possible, listing each behavior, action, or interaction by using clear, action-based descriptions.

_____

_____

_____

_____

_____

Who first noticed that things had changed? Who else noticed?

_____

_____

_____

_____

When did you first notice that things had begun to change? What did you notice happening at that time? Be as specific as possible, listing each behavior, action, or interaction by using clear, action-based descriptions.

_____

_____

_____

_____

_____

How did the change happen? What did you do? What did your son or daughter do? What did others do? Be as specific as possible, listing each behavior, action, or interaction by using clear, action-based descriptions.

_____

_____

_____

_____

_____

How did you get yourself to do what you did?

_____

_____

_____

_____

_____

How was what you did different than what you've done in the past?

_____

_____

_____

_____

_____

How has the change been helpful to you? To your son or daughter? To your family?

_____

_____

_____

_____

_____

What will be different in the future as these changes continue?

_____

_____

_____

_____

_____

Who else might benefit from these changes? How so?

_____

_____

_____

_____

_____

Bring this sheet to your next session and discuss it with your therapist, and/or talk about it with your son or daughter and/or family.

69

What Is It About You?

THERAPIST'S OVERVIEW

Purpose of Exercise

When change has occurred it's important that clients attribute the majority of that change to their internal qualities and actions. If clients attribute the bulk of change to external factors (e.g., medication, therapists, etc.), when those external factors diminish in their effectiveness in the eyes of clients or others, the change also tends to diminish. Outcome research has indicated that persistent change correlates strongly with clients' attribution of change to something about themselves.

The purpose of this exercise is to help parents, children, and adolescents attribute change to their own personal qualities or actions. To do this, clients are assisted in identifying their roles in change processes and in taking credit for those changes. This can help to extend those changes into the future.

Suggestions for Use

1. This exercise can be used with parents, children, and adolescents.
2. When asked how change occurred, many children and adolescents will respond with, "I don't know." Don't be phased by this. You may respond with "So you don't know how you made this happen." This acknowledges the client's view and suggests that the client had some influence on the change. Continue to hold out the possibility that they had something to do with those changes.
3. With responses such as "I don't know" it can also be helpful to speculate about change. For example, with an adolescent you might say, "I wonder if change has occurred in part because you're growing up and getting a little older and a little wiser." With a parent you might say, "I wonder if your hard work is paying off and that parenting is starting to take hold a little better." Choose things that clients are unlikely to discount.
4. Even when medication or some other external factor has had an effect on positive change, find out what that external factor allowed that person to do, thereby letting him or her know that he or she still took some action. For example, with an adolescent who is taking medication you might say, "What has the medication allowed you to do that you might not have otherwise done?"

EXERCISE

When change occurs, even though it can seem as if other factors have brought about that change, it is often helpful to frame all change with humans as self-change. It requires action on the part of people. Even though external factors such as medication and therapy can help people, they only facilitate change. Ultimately, you, your son or daughter, or some other family member had to do something to bring about that change. Yet even when it is difficult to identify what happened, you can still look with yourself and your family members to explore internal qualities that allowed change to happen. This exercise will help you identify what it is about you or others that allowed change to occur.

To complete this exercise, write your responses to the questions in the spaces provided.

1. What did you do to make your situation better with the problem you've been facing? Be specific.

_____

_____

_____

_____

_____

2. What other kinds of things helped (e.g., medication, your therapist, therapy, friends, etc.) with change happening in regard to the problem you've been facing? Please list these things.

1. _____

2. _____

3. _____

4. _____

5. _____

3. Who helped you with the problem that you've been facing? How did they help you? List each person and how he or she helped you.

1. _____

2. _____

3. _____

4. _____

5. _____

4. What did those things you listed in question #2 and the help of others (question #3) allow you to do that you might not have otherwise done?

_____

_____

_____

_____

_____

5. What is it about you as a person that made it possible to face up to the problem you've been dealing with?

_____

_____

_____

_____

_____

6. If you are unsure as to what it is about you that has helped you face the problem, consider some of the following changes that you may have experienced:

- I'm becoming wiser.
- I'm growing as a person.
- I've learned more about myself, which has helped me deal with adversity.
- I'm better at dealing with life's trials and tribulations.

Do any of these changes ring true to you? If so, which one(s)? If not, what other possible changes might you consider?

_____

_____

_____

_____

_____

Continue to consider what it is that you may have done and/or what it says about you as a person that you've been able to stand up to the problems you've been facing.

70

Is It Enough? Reviewing Change

THERAPIST'S OVERVIEW

Purpose of Exercise

When change has occurred it's important to determine whether that change indicates resolution of the problem or whether further change is necessary. The purpose of this exercise is to assist therapists and clients in determining how the change they've experienced developed in relation to the goals and preferred outcomes that have been established.

Suggestions for Use

1. This exercise can be used with parents, children, and adolescents.
2. It's important to hear from each person involved, and his or her view of how the change that has occurred relates to the overall goals that have been established.
3. This exercise can help therapists and clients. Keep in mind, if you don't know where you're going you'll probably end up somewhere else. Therefore, we want to know how progress that has been made relates to goals and preferred outcomes.

EXERCISE

When change has occurred, it's important to determine how that change relates to the problem you've been facing as well as the goals and preferred outcomes that you've established. This exercise will help you figure out whether the change you've experienced is sufficient enough to consider the problem resolved and if not, what else needs to occur for you to feel that the problem is no longer a problem.

To complete this exercise, write your responses to the questions in the spaces provided.

How are you/your child or adolescent/family benefiting from the changes you've experienced?

_____

_____

_____

_____

_____

How does the change that's happened relate to the goals that you set?

_____

_____

_____

_____

_____

On a scale of 1 to 10, with 1 representing "not at all" and 10 representing "totally," to what degree have the goals that you set been met? Be specific by listing a number and describing how well your goals have been met.

_____

_____

_____

_____

_____

On a scale of 1 to 10, with 1 representing "not at all" and 10 representing "totally," rate your level of confidence that you now have the tools to continue to maintain progress toward your goal. What has happened that gives you confidence?

_____

_____

_____

_____

_____

What else, if anything, needs to happen to fade this problem from your life?

_____

_____

_____

_____

_____

What would be a first step indicating that this problem is fading further from your life?

_____

_____

_____

_____

_____

71

Recovering from Setbacks

THERAPIST'S OVERVIEW

Purpose of the Exercise

There is no such thing as a problem-free life. Everyone experiences difficulty at one time or another. Setbacks do not necessarily mark a return to stage one. In fact, sometimes change that lasts is more like three steps forward, two steps back. What is important is how clients respond to setbacks.

The purpose of this exercise is to help clients manage setbacks in their lives. It is designed to help clients use their internal and external resources to get back on track.

Suggestions for Use

1. This exercise can be used with parents and adolescents.
2. It can be helpful to talk with families about the idea of a family life cycle. That is, families experience different difficulties at different times in life. For example, the kinds of problems that parents face with young children are typically different than those with teenagers.
3. It can be helpful to frame setbacks as time for adjustments and tweaking. This helps clients to keep doing what is working and doing away with what is not. Also consider using the "three steps forward, two steps back" metaphor if it fits for clients.

EXERCISE

We have all learned that life is not problem free. In addition, even when we have made progress toward goals, there are times when we have temporary setbacks. These setbacks or lapses do not necessarily mean a return to the old, full-blown problem. Instead, they are indications that some of what we are doing is working and some is not. Setbacks mark times of adjustment and tweaking. This exercise will help you recover from setbacks you face and get back on track.

To complete this exercise, fill in your answers in the spaces provided.

When the problem reappeared, how did you manage to keep it from getting any worse?

_____

_____

_____

_____

_____

How did you think to do what you did?

_____

_____

_____

_____

_____

Who else, if anyone, was around to help bring the setback to an end? How did he/she/they help?

_____

_____

_____

_____

_____

What have you learned from this setback? How can that be helpful to you in the future?

_____

_____

_____

_____

How can that be helpful in the future should you face a similar or different type of setback?

_____

_____

_____

_____

_____

What needs to happen for things to get back on track? What specifically will you do?

_____

_____

_____

_____

_____

72

Managing Ups and Downs

THERAPIST'S OVERVIEW

Purpose of the Exercise

In any relationship there are bound to be ups and downs. Recovering from difficulties is an important relationship skill. The problem is not that parents differ from their children and adolescents in important ways but rather, what they do with those differences. Clients frequently seem to approach their sessions as an opportunity to complain about a recent disagreement with a family member. If the therapist does not intervene, the session can easily escalate into accusations and placing of blame. However, if the topic can be turned to a discussion of conversational patterns and how to make them more effective, there is the possibility that more effective patterns can be developed. This exercise is designed for use by the client between sessions to encourage self-evaluation and new behaviors.

Suggestions for Use

1. This exercise can be used with parents and adults.
2. In the session, it can be helpful to have clients work through a recent problem interaction before suggesting this exercise. Then suggest that they can do it on their own.
3. Avoid assigning blame and turn the focus to future successful interactions.

EXERCISE

Disagreements are an unavoidable part of any relationship. In and of themselves, they are not a problem. The important question is how you handle differences with others. This exercise is designed to help you think about interactions that have been unacceptable to you and make the most of them.

To complete this exercise, fill in your answers in the spaces provided.

Recall a recent disagreement with your child or adolescent. Describe exactly what happened. Be as precise as possible about what was said and done and in what order.

_____

_____

_____

_____

_____

_____

_____

_____

_____

_____

Look over your description and mark your parts of the interaction. Next, list three things that you were trying to accomplish.

1. _____

2. _____

3. _____

Then, examine your contributions to the interaction and find at least three things you could have done that would have made the interaction go differently without sacrificing your motivations.

List three things that you can learn from this interaction.

1. _____

2. _____

3. _____

In the future, what will tip you off that you are entering an interaction where you can try something different?

_____

_____

_____

_____

_____

What specifically will you do differently?

_____

_____

_____

_____

_____

How will you know you are making progress?

_____

_____

_____

_____

_____

73

The Scrapbook of Life

THERAPIST'S OVERVIEW

Purpose of the Exercise

As children grow up, many parents keep scrapbooks of their children's and adolescent's accomplishments. Others keep papers with good marks and display them in their homes where others can see them. Still others frame certificates and photos of graduations. All of these, as well as other acts by parents, highlight the accomplishments of their sons and daughters. This is important in sharing the stories of success and of growing up of young people. In a similar way, parents can keep scrapbooks or keep track of their sons' and daughters' progress in standing up to and overcoming obstacles and difficulties.

The purpose of this exercise is threefold. First, it helps children and adolescents focus on positive future change and doing the behaviors that their parents are seeking. Second, it shares the stories of these children and adolescents with others, thereby strengthening the new, valued story. Third, simply by looking at their "collections of success," children and adolescents can be reminded of their accomplishments, how they are changing, previous solutions, and what they are capable of.

Suggestions for Use

1. This exercise is applicable with children and adolescents. It will be up to those involved to decide what the best way is of documenting change.
2. As much as possible, involve children and adolescents in tracking and documenting accomplishments.
3. Be sure to have children and adolescents periodically review their scrapbooks to remind them of their changes and successes.

Note: This exercise can be paired with, "Where's the Evidence?"

EXERCISE

Many of us have had the experience of going though personal scrapbooks and in reexperiencing our accomplishments. Others of us have had assignments that we've done well on posted on the refrigerator or shown to relatives. Growing up, you may have even had your name in the paper for being on the honor roll, for graduation, for being successful in school sports, for being part of a club, and so on. These types of recognition can make a difference to struggling children and adolescents. A little recognition can go a long way.

This exercise will help you track and document, along with your son or daughter, the successes that he or she has had and the changes that have occurred. In the form of a scrapbook (or other alternative means if you choose), you will maintain a record of your son's or daughter's accomplishments. This can help in at least three ways. First, it can help your son or daughter to focus on positive future change and doing the behaviors that you are seeking. Second, it shares your son's or daughter's success story with others, thereby strengthening the new, valued story. Third, simply by looking at his or her "collections of success," your son or daughter can be reminded of his or her accomplishments, how he or she is changing, previous solutions, and what he or she is capable of.

To complete this exercise, follow the directions.

With your son or daughter, purchase, find, or create a scrapbook. You may choose to buy one from a store or use an extra notebook or binder you have lying around. You may also choose to create one by using cardboard or card stock or other materials you have access to.

If you wish, decorate the cover by adding artwork, pictures, photos, and/or your son's or daughter's name.

Put the date on the front cover, inside cover, or the first page of the scrapbook so you know when it was started.

Talk with your son or daughter about the kinds of things that will be included in the scrapbook. These should be things that mark successes, accomplishments, and progress toward problems or difficulties. List those things that will be included in the scrapbook in the spaces provided. Be open to adding or modifying this list as you find new things that should be added.

1. _____

2. _____

3. _____

4. _____

5. _____

6. _____

7. _____

8. _____

9. _____

10. _____

When a piece of evidence that represents a success, accomplishment, and/or progress toward a problem or difficulty is identified, along with your son or daughter, set aside a time to put that evidence into the scrapbook.

Make sure that at least two times per week you set time aside with your son or daughter to review the scrapbook and to talk about the changes that he or she has made. Here are some questions to consider asking:

- How did you accomplish what you did?
- What steps did you take?
- How did you approach the situation differently than you had in the past?
- What else needs to happen to keep the change going?
- What can I do to help you? Others?

Make sure that the scrapbook is out in the open where others can look at it.

74

Certifiably Changed

Purpose of the Exercise

When children and adolescents have overcome difficulties and problems it can be helpful to celebrate those changes with a certificate of accomplishment. This is consistent with schools, clubs, sports, and programs that mark completion, successes, accomplishments, and the reaching of goals with certificates.

The purpose of this exercise is to help children and younger adolescents celebrate their accomplishments. Certificates can symbolize success, overcoming obstacles, or mark the transition into the future. This can help children and younger adolescents with their sense of self and self-esteem. It can also help them to further use their strengths and abilities by recognizing that they have had some success in the past.

Suggestions for Use

1. This exercise will be most applicable to children and younger adolescents. Older adolescents are likely to be less interested in the idea and may wish to celebrate accomplishments in other ways or not at all.
2. Certificates are easy to make. They can be created by hand or on a computer.
3. Use certificates only for special accomplishments. If they are used too frequently, their effectiveness will be diluted.
4. Therapists or parents can create certificates.

EXERCISE

When children and adolescents have made changes and overcome problems, it's important to recognize those changes and celebrate them. For children and younger adolescents, one way of doing this is to use certificates to signify accomplishment. This exercise will help you to create certificates to mark positive changes that have occurred with your son or daughter or to celebrate some success. This can help with his or her sense of self and self-esteem. It can also help your son or daughter to further use his or her strengths and abilities by recognizing that he or she has had some success in the past.

To complete this exercise, follow the directions.

Identify the problem that your son or daughter has overcome.

Determine what skills were involved in overcoming that problem. Be specific and use behavioral descriptions. List the skills in the spaces provided.

1. _____

2. _____

3. _____

4. _____

5. _____

6. _____

7. _____

8. _____

9. _____

10. _____

Now it's time to get creative. Give the primary new skill a name (e.g., The Tantrum Tamer, Overcoming Anger, etc.).

_____

Create a certificate. For examples, refer to the following pages.

Present the certificate to your son or daughter.

CERTIFICATE OF ACHIEVEMENT

This certificate is hereby awarded to

Tim Johnson

On this day, September 1st, 2001
For demonstrating his ability to tame tantrums

Bob Bertolino
Bob Bertolino, PhD

CERTIFICATE OF CHANGE

This certificate is hereby awarded to

Laurie Waters

On this day, September 1st, 2001
For success in standing up to anger
and for
Getting her life back

Mom & Dad

CERTIFICATE
OF
ACHIEVEMENT

This certificate is hereby awarded to

_____

On this day, _____

For demonstrating _____ ability to face up to

_____

_____

CERTIFICATE
OF
CHANGE

This certificate is hereby awarded to

_____

On this day, _____

For success in standing up to

_____

and for

Getting _____ **life back**

_____

75

Facing the Future

THERAPIST'S OVERVIEW

Purpose of the Exercise

Once a problem has been overcome it can be helpful to work with parents, children, and adolescents to identify how they will extend those changes into the future. In addition, therapists can prepare clients in dealing with other problems, present or future, by orienting them toward those abilities that they have used in the past. This can serve as a form of relapse prevention.

The purpose of this exercise is to help parents, children, and adolescents identify possible future impediments to change and to utilize their new learnings and skills to stand up to such challenges.

Suggestions for Use

1. This exercise is applicable to parents, children, and adolescents.
2. It's a good idea to tell clients that they *might* face the same or similar problems again, not that they *will* face the same ones.
3. Suggest to clients that they already have the skills that they need to face future adversity.

EXERCISE

This exercise will help your family to extend the changes that you've made into the future. This way, you can continue to grow and attain the futures that you prefer. It will also help you use what you've learned in facing up to problems that might arise in the future—whether they are similar or different ones. Then, you will be more prepared to deal with any adversity that might arise.

To complete this exercise, write your responses to the questions in the spaces provided.

What will you be doing to continue the changes you've made into the future?

_____

_____

_____

_____

_____

What will be different as a result of your actions?

_____

_____

_____

_____

_____

What do you need from others to keep things moving forward?

_____

_____

_____

_____

_____

What might be an indication to you that the problem was attempting to resurface? What might be the first sign?

_____

_____

_____

_____

_____

What will you do differently in the future if faced with the same or a similar problem?

_____

_____

_____

_____

_____

How can what you've learned be of help to you in solving future problems?

_____

_____

_____

_____

_____

If you feel yourself slipping, what's one thing that can stop that slipping and get you back on track?

_____

_____

_____

_____

_____

Keep this sheet available should you need to refer back to it.

Index

Page numbers followed by the letter "f" indicate a figure.

5 easy ways to order!

 PHONE
1.800.429.6784
Outside US/Canada: 607.722.5857

 FAX
1.800.895.0582
Outside US/Canada: 607.771.0012

 E-MAIL
orders@haworthpressinc.com

 WEB
www.HaworthPress.com

MAIL
The Haworth Press, Inc.
10 Alice Street
Binghamton, NY 13904-1580 USA

❑ **YES!** Please rush me the following book(s)

❶ ❑ **The Therapist's Notebook**
Homework, Handouts, and Activities for Use in Psychotherapy

❑ $49.95 soft. ISBN: 0-7890-0400-3 _____ **Quantity**

Order this book online at: www.HaworthPressInc.com/store/product.asp?sku=1567

❷ ❑ **The Therapist's Notebook for Children and Adolescents**
Homework, Handouts, and Activities for Use in Psychotherapy

❑ $39.95 soft. ISBN: 0-7890-1096-8 _____ **Quantity**

Order this book online at: www.HaworthPressInc.com/store/product.asp?sku=4742

❸ ❑ **The Therapist's Notebook for Families**
Solution-Oriented Exercises for Working with Parents, Children, and Adolescents

❑ $39.95 soft. ISBN: 0-7890-1244-8 _____ **Quantity**

Order this book online at: www.HaworthPressInc.com/store/product.asp?sku=4645

❹ ❑ **The Therapist's Notebook for Lesbian, Gay, and Bisexual Clients**
Homework, Handouts, and Activities for Use in Psychotherapy

❑ $39.95 soft. ISBN: 0-7890-1252-9 _____ **Quantity**

Order this book online at: www.HaworthPressInc.com/store/product.asp?sku=4743

Order Today!

PAYMENT OPTIONS

❑ **BILL ME LATER.** ($5.00 service charge will be added.) (Not available on individual orders outside US/Canada/Mexico. Minimum order: $15. Service charge is waived for jobbers/wholesalers/booksellers.)

P.O.# _____

Signature _____

❑ **PAYMENT ENCLOSED. $** _____
Payment by check or money order must be in U.S. or Canadian dollars drawn on a U.S. or Canadian bank.

❑ **PLEASE CHARGE TO MY CREDIT CARD:**
❑ Visa ❑ MasterCard ❑ AmEx ❑ Discover ❑ Diners Club ❑ Eurocard ❑ JCB

Account _____

Exp. Date _____

Signature _____

May we open a confidential credit card account for you for possible future purchases? ❑ Yes ❑ No

FINAL TALLIES

		POSTAGE AND HANDLING:	
COST OF BOOK(S)		**If your book total is:**	**Add this amount:**
		up to $29.95	$5.00
POSTAGE & HANDLING See chart at right.		$30.00 – $49.99	$6.00
		$50.00 – $69.99	$7.00
		$70.00 – $89.99	$8.00
IN CANADA Please add 7% for GST. NFLD, NS, NB: Add 8% for province tax.		$90.00 – $109.99	$9.00
		$110.00 – $129.99	$10.00
		$130.00 – $149.99	$11.00
		$150.00 – and up	$12.00
State Tax NY, OH & MN add local sales tax.		US orders will be shipped via UPS; Outside US orders will be shipped via Book Printed Matter. For shipments via other delivery services, contact Haworth for details. Allow 3–4 weeks for delivery after publication. Based on US dollars. Booksellers: Call for freight charges.	
FINAL TOTAL			

- If paying in Canadian funds, please use the current exchange rate. Payment in UNESCO coupons welcome.
- Individual orders outside the US/Canada/Mexico must be prepaid by check or credit card.
- Prices in US dollars and subject to change without notice.

ADDITIONAL INFORMATION

Please fill in the information below or **TAPE YOUR BUSINESS CARD IN THIS AREA.**

NAME _____

INSTITUTION _____

ADDRESS _____

_____

CITY _____

STATE/PROVINCE _____

ZIP/POSTAL CODE _____

COUNTY (NY Residents only) _____

COUNTRY _____

PHONE _____

FAX _____

E-MAIL _____

PLEASE PRINT OR TYPE CLEARLY.
May we use your e-mail address for confirmations and other types of information? ❑ Yes ❑ No
We appreciate receiving your e-mail address and fax number. Haworth would like to e-mail or fax special discount offers to you, as a preferred customer. We will **never share, rent, or exchange** your e-mail address or fax number. We regard such actions as an invasion of your privacy.

THIS FORM MAY BE PHOTOCOPIED FOR DISTRIBUTION.

Order from your local bookstore or directly from
The Haworth Press, Inc.
10 Alice Street • Binghamton, New York 13904–1580 • USA
Telephone: 1.800.429.6784 • Fax: 1.800.895.0582
Outside US/Canada: Telephone: 607.722.5857 • Fax: 607.771.0012
E-mail: orders@haworthpressinc.com

Visit our website at: www.HaworthPress.com ▸

CODE: BOF02